I0437874

IN SEARCH OF THE DISPLACED PERSONS

Andy Evans and Vesna Kovac

authorHOUSE®

AuthorHouse™ UK Ltd.
500 Avebury Boulevard
Central Milton Keynes, MK9 2BE
www.authorhouse.co.uk
Phone: 08001974150

© 2009 Andy Evans and Vesna Kovac. All rights reserved.

No part of this book may be reproduced, stored in a retrieval system, or transmitted by any means without the written permission of the author.

First published by AuthorHouse 6/19/2009

ISBN: 978-1-4389-9882-4 (sc)

This book is printed on acid-free paper.

About the Authors

Andy Evans was born in the gritty coal mining communities of West Yorkshire England.

After leaving school at the age of sixteen he followed the generations of school leavers before him to work in the local coal mines.

Following the demise of the coal mining industry he now works within the Criminal Justice System.

Andy is married with two children and has a granddaughter, Ava. He continues to live in his native West Yorkshire.

Vesna Kovac was born and raised in her homeland of Bosnia. After leaving school she went onto graduate as an engineer at the Military Academy in Zagreb, Croatia and went onto work at the Bratstvo Armaments factory in Novi Travnik. She remained in Bosnia until the end of the war and now lives in the USA with her husband and two sons.

The book is dedicated to the everlasting memories of Maksim Ćulumović (Ćulum) and Petra Pljuco without whom none of the words would have been possible.

Maksim Ćulumović (Ćulum)
1909 - 1988

Petra Pljuco
1935 - 2007

Acknowledgements and Thanks

Special thanks to the following for all the kind help and time given throughout my endless search to;

Segeij and the kind people of the Serbian Genealogical Society / Srpsko Rodoslovno Društvo

Roko – For all of your help and patience which finally paid off with you making the final connection which enabled me to proceed and succeed in my search.

Vanja – Whose kind parents travelled to Brdani on my behalf and made the final connection.

Contents

Prologue

THE FOLLOWING PAGES GIVE AN account of a twenty year search to uncover the mystery that had surrounded grandfather for the entirety of his life that he had spent living in the United Kingdom. All that was ever known of him were the basic facts that he was Serbian by nationality (although I was later to discover that he in fact lived in Bosnia) and that he was never to return to his native homeland again.

The book is like that of a split personality, two sides that would never see the other until the final chapters were acknowledged, recorded and written together.

It describes my own early recollections of the man and the time I would spend in his presence throughout childhood and teenage years until his death in 1988.

The other persona tells of the other side that was left behind in Bosnia. The happiness, ever wandering, the horrors and finally, as the first one is uncovered, the understanding and joining together of both as finally one.

The search would be a relentless task searching for a man that had no records of his existence prior to his displacement in 1946. Searching a country whose own bloodlust and carnage has seen whole generations of people and records of them disappear forever. A country whose varied people are so secretive in their own right and often hide their own pasts with a passion.

It would see me travel to Bosnia only to be faced with the realisation that nothing there could be found.

Private Investigators that specialised in genealogy would be hired but it would be by sheer chance that the mystery would eventually unfold and a family lost for over sixty years would be uncovered.

A second visit to Bosnia would result in reunion and embrace and it would become clear that the connection had not been lost but was merely lying dormant in the passing of time.

The stories would begin to unfold from both sides, so differently told. Stories and memories so very different but would have the magnetic pull that would keep them connected without each knowing of the others existence. The same memories would become entwined spiritually as if they had never been apart.

Two lost brothers that had known of the others continued existence but for reasons out of their control would never have any contact for over sixty years until their deaths twelve months apart.

The connection would continue and would increase its pull even after their deaths and would eventually draw both sides together with a clarity that would have the feeling that they had never been apart.

Two separate people that had never met but found themselves spiritually drawn together with one goal. Finally, to bridge the gap that had been suspended for so long and to record finally the years that had been lost.

Chapter One – Early Years from Memory

The End of the Beginning

FOLLOWING THE COMPLETE CEASEFIRE OF hostilities in war ravaged Europe many hundreds of thousands of refugees found themselves displaced from their native homelands. Return to their irrespective country to most would often lead to persecution, torture and possible execution. The reasons were many but the most probable cause was that they had simply fought to protect their people and homelands from the occupying German forces and, as these were pushed back, the newly emerging communist regimes that were being heavily supported by the encroaching Soviet army and which were to replace centuries old, exiting regimes and reshape Europe for over half a decade.

Although the stories are countless and come from every country once caught under the impregnable grip of the former iron curtain my own centres on the now independent countries of the former Yugoslavia. Fifty year old stories of horror and suffering for its varied people have since been replaced with fresh horrors from the unimaginable carnage and bloodlust which erupted in the 1990's and this has weighed enormously in my own relentless quest for information.

My own search focuses on one individual who gave me so much in my early years that the memories will stay entwined in my being for eternity. There is not one memory from my childhood that does not escape his ever presence and even today, twenty years after his death, his influence and advice still fill my everyday life. Looking back a lot of this intrigue was centred on the never ending secrecy that seemed to follow him wherever he went. A man of very few words before what appeared to be his miraculous appearance on earth in 1946 at the birth age of thirty seven he seemed to me, as a child the very fabric of hidden knowledge and deep understanding. A very being that would draw those around him to the enveloping mystery and never knowing that he was so much a part of, the fact that this deep and impenetrable mist could never be breached always added to the inner rooted loyalty and connection that has stayed with me to this very day.

My search as been extensive to say the least. From humble beginnings following his death in 1988 to the use of Private Investigators, Hand Writing specialists and hours of searching internet files and posting countless appeals on genealogical websites. Never endless days had drawn me to the conclusion that my search would never be answered and so many times I have held my head in despair the realisation that my efforts would be inconclusive, that I searched for a man that had never existed only in this country from 1946. Steps taken forewords, sleepwalking back again always seemed the order of the day, I would make progress only to face the stark realisation days later that the path I had chosen was leading me to unknown ground and that the facts did not necessary tally with what I already knew from memory, research and common sense.

The following pages not only detail the exhausting search but give an insight into what had been my driving force to uncover the veiled truth of a mans existence. From my humble beginnings being raised in a grim Yorkshire mining village where coal was king and every essence of life centred on the colliery, to my visits to Bosnia and finally lifting the veil that had evaded me for twenty years of searching. There are stories from both sides of the coin, my own recollections of a childhood spent with a man so obviously alien to his surroundings to recollections of lost people spending the same years in their native land of Bosnia. Each side of the coin would never know of the others existence until the search was finalised and the passing of time would be at last embraced with reunion some sixty years after the coin was tossed for the very first time.

My Little Town

Featherstone is a town within the Wakefield District, in West Yorkshire, England and lies south west of Pontefract and has a population of 16,375

Like many towns in the area, it grew around Coal Mining, and was the site of a miners' Strike in 1893. During the strike the town came to national attention when soldiers fired on striking miners killing two. A distinctive sculpture marking the centenary of the Featherstone Massacre stands in the shopping precinct and a large mural depicting the town's heritage can be seen at the town's main crossroads. Ackton Hall Colliery was the first pit to close following the end of the miners' strike and this could not be contested as geological difficulties had made it impossible for the pit to continue production.

Despite most population growth taking place around the Industrial Revolution, Featherstone traces its history back much further than this. It is thought that a local public house, the Travellers Rest, can trace its origins to the 17th century whilst the Jubilee Hotel is a listed building which once provided a resting place for wealthy Victorians and their horses.

Sparrows Chirping and Rain Drops Falling

It always rains on a Sunday I would say to myself as I looked out of the window. 7 am and already woken by the sounds of granddad busying himself and making breakfast, usually cheese and fresh eggs (laid within the hour) cooked to perfection in the coal fired Yorkshire stove.

Sparrows always fascinated me as I looked out of the window overlooking the front houses of Gladstone Street. They would busy themselves in their daily lives, seemingly oblivious to the rigors of everyday life in my little town. They would hurriedly feed their young chicks with scraps offered from many of the houses left over breakfast tables. Bacon rind and bread – Sparrows in my generation seemed to live a very unhealthy lifestyle of fatty foods. How they flew I do not know to this day.

Its strange how one memory in particular stays embedded in your mind for no particular reason and will manifest itself whenever the strange tricks of the human mind automatically regress with flicker images of ones outstanding existence. A catastrophic event that I could recall would be welcomed in adult conversation on childhood memories but no, sparrows, rainfall and bacon rind will always, I fear be the essence of my early years.

There are many books today written about local history, especially the sprawling expanses of the northern mining communities which were the heart and soul of Britain's prosperity. My own story, in its beginning will merely scratch on the surface of this proud heritage which is now in its final throes of demise, but will focus on a primary socialization which changed the course of events entirely for myself as I developed and which fuelled the fires for the need to pen these chapters and seek the truth finally.

Featherstone today is a far away place as it was merely forty two years ago when my own eyes opened for the very first time. To have skin other than white meant that that the holder had not bathed in the pit head baths following his working day at the colliery and any foreign language would be associated with the speaker being from a neighbouring county, here to reap the rewards of the promising wages of the prospering

Yorkshire coalfield..

My recollections of childhood were those of happy times. Featherstone seemed like a warm pillow of protection which I embraced and comforted in its warm and happy people. Everyone seemed to help each other, knew each other and cared for each other. I recall even funerals, fondly as a child; the whole street seemed to have a certain "buzz" on the particular morning. Women would scrub the steps and immediate street surface with hot soapy water and clean away any traces of grime before the cortège appeared, in respect for the sad passing of a dear neighbour. It almost seemed like a competition – who had the cleanest steps to be remembered for eternity by the loving departed.

Childhood memories are filled with endless days of self taught amusement where games often transpired from imagination and would then be adapted with the passing of time to ensure they were the latest trends and fashionable. Hide and seek, kick out can and the constant re-enactment of fiercely fought Hollywood battles between warring factions from World War Two were always popular and afforded hours and days of rich amusement.

Looking back now it is sad to see the once favourite haunts of endless generations of happy, go lucky children now deserted and derelict. Short cuts and woodland have now receded back to the clutches of nature as hurriedly running feet now tend to stay within the confines of relative safety within the street lit paths and streets, computers and gaming stations have replaced the plastic rifles and empty aluminium cans and the gathering of adolescents on street corners is now frowned upon and seen more of an annoyance. From today's modern standards I guess we were poor people but most importantly we were happy people. Looking back now I feel it was so nice to be poor in retrospect.

Like many northern coal mining towns Featherstone was lacking in amenities to say the least. Public Houses and Working Men's Clubs were the prominent feature of leisure time and were usually busy centres for the local community.

The younger generations were catered for in the many sporting activities in the form of Rugby League, Soccer and Cricket.

The more senior residents tended to take solace in the many stretches of available plots of land, or allotments as these were known, to make good use of and to enjoy the fresh air and be a respite away from the harsh reality of coal mining.

These plots of land were usually the pride and joy of the allotment keeper, vegetables and fruits were grown as well as poultry rearing and the often obsessive sport of pigeon racing were catered for.

Grandfather's particular allotment or plot of land will be another deeply embedded chapter in the annals of my particular memories from both my primary and secondary socialization.

Maybe it never actually always rained on a Sunday because I spent so much time there, it was always sunshine. The air would be filled with the song of the Skylark from neighbouring farmland and the shrieks of dismay always followed from the disturbed Blackbird.

Like many northern coal mining towns Featherstone was lacking in amenities to say the least. Public Houses and Working Men's Clubs were the prominent feature of leisure time and were usually busy centres for the local community.

Grandfather's space was so different. Usually these allotments were a mish mash of collective junk – old doors as fences and lack lustre attempts at keeping nature's wild growth at bay.

Whenever you entered this space you were transformed away from the grit and grime of Featherstone. This was Alice Through The looking Glass without the novel. Everything was transformed to a different place, so alien to its surroundings. The collection of huts and sheds were constructed in a way that I would not see again until my recent journey to Bosnia.

Everything in this magical place was done to such an high

standard and perfection, so unlike its neighbouring plots. You entered through a panelled door which cut through a boundary hedge, always trimmed to exact straight lines. Hedges were always a target for us as children and would leap into them with childish frenzy to be ejected at speed with the force of there natural ability to spring back into place. Not this hedge. It, for some reason was never targeted. It was "Max's hedge" and was avoided at all cost.

Once through the door it would fascinate me each time just how perfect everything was kept. Everything was carefully planned from the grassed path that ran in a straight line central to the plots of vegetables, to the boundary fences.

Everything was grown here from the native vegetables of England to tobacco. Never before nor have I since seen tobacco plants grown in this country.

The leaves would be harvested in late summer and hung to dry in the wooden huts, giving off a pungent odour that at times I can still occasionally smell today as I enter a room.

The crowning glory to me as a child would have to be the huge greenhouse that I would fondly call the Crystal Palace due to it imposing construction. This must have been twenty meters in length by eight meters in width and was heated by water pipes fed from a coal burning stove.

Tomatoes grown here were renowned for their flavour and summer school holidays for me were spent selling these door to door from a huge wooden wheelbarrow. I recall that the demand for these always outweighed and the wheelbarrow always emptied faster than it could be restocked with carefully weighed produce. Grandfather is still fondly remembered by the more senior residents for the tomatoes he produced.

Many memories stay ingrained from childhood and these are simply ripples from the surface that immediately rise to the forefront whenever I think back to his life. What I do recall is an individual that seemed to stand out from any crowd that he was part of and who seemed to summon respect amongst his own nationals which reinforced the whole secrecy surrounding him.

Children would offer him the same respect and be on their best behaviour whenever he was in their presence. Strangely as my research drew to a close it was interesting to find that the brother who had survived in Bosnia had the same traits and characteristics despite the two having been cut apart some forty years before their deaths.

Simple forms of identical body language, how they stood and held their arms to the preference of how they would wear their hats all appeared to survive the passing of time and remained part of the very essence that was brotherhood and a connection that remained so deeply embedded into their very fabric that isolation from each other had survived.

Chapter Two – Steps Taken Forewords Sleepwalking Back Again

Induction and Isolation

FEATHERSTONE IN THE LATE **1940's** would have been a very foreboding and miserable place even for it's native inhabitants socialised from birth to a life of Victorian squalor and Coal Mining.

Displaced refugees were eagerly accepted by the post war government to replace the labour force that had perished in the war and any individual would be seen as simply that, a worker to replace one that was no longer there.

Exploitation was here on a grand scale. The displaced refugees from war torn Europe simply had no choice, either accept the stringent conditions set out by the host government or simply return to their native countries and face possible death. Life can deal at times a cruel hand and this was the hand of all games played with human life that my own country participated.

Life for a life here literally meant that. Three year contracts were signed by the Ministry of Labour were sealed, either the participant honoured their three year contract of designated work or they would be returned, immediately to their respective homelands.

Coal mining was king here so coal miners were needed to hue the coals. This was regardless of experience in the industry so it would appear that simply cattle were sent to graze the offered pasture.

The newcomers to our country were met with obvious glee from the newly Nationalised Coal Industry who had a seemingly endless supply of green labour to fulfil their demands to fuel Britain's economy once more following hostilities..

Upon arrival in the UK from displaced persons camps in Italy and Germany the arrivals were then dispersed into the many camps that had been hurriedly readied for them across the country.

Maksim was inducted into Full Sutton Camp near the city of York in Yorkshire. The camp like many others had been crudely planned and the DP's were made up of many different nationals from across Europe. Little or no thought had been given to the huge differences between the individuals there and devout enemies were placed together, maybe hoping that with the world at peace, old feuds would be forgotten. It is interesting to read that during one sitting in the House of Commons a debate took place regarding the behaviour towards each other of the displaced persons at Full Sutton Camp. Strangely too that the only photograph in my possession of grandfather at this camp that he has obvious bruising to his left eye.

At Full Sutton he was processed by the Ministry of Labour and like many others he was designated to work in the coal mining industry. He was learnt basic English and then dispatched again to a Miners Hostel at Askern in South Yorkshire where he underwent the very basics of training required to work underground at Askern Colliery. Once this short cut training was complete he was again moved to the miner's hostel at High Town in Castleford within two miles of the designated colliery at Fryston, on the outer fringes of Castleford.

Kicking Around on a Piece of Ground.....

As the slow passing of childhood years changed gear and seemed to accelerate away from me I found myself becoming more and more intrigued in the man that had played a central role in my early upbringing. As teenage years beckoned I would spend more and more time around the man that I looked to and respected so much. Granddad "Max", it was obvious to me, found great solace in the fact that here was a kid that not only held so much adoration for him but also wanted so badly to be included in the very fabric of his life. At times it felt to me that I was being moulded to represent cherished ones from a family long since gone, never to return from a land so far away and unknown to me. I knew the part I was to play and was happy that this had been offered to me from a figure in my life that I adored so much and respected that this was how it should be.

Maybe the fuelling fires to this deeply rooted connection we held was the very unknowing that seemed to envelope him in a veiled mist of never knowing the man entirely as he had been and could never be again. To be displaced entirely from your natural surroundings must be the cruellest blow ever to be experienced, life is built on experience and memory, to have these taken away must be like having the very soul of your existence torn out and replaced with a blank page of knowing nothing, only what could have been.

Here was a man that had arrived in the United Kingdom in 1946 at the birth age of thirty six years. Nothing gave his story away prior to this overdue birth, neither fond recollections nor anecdotal stories of youth and happiness told to amuse the audience over food and drink. Here was a mystery man that had simply no past that could be continued to create a continued line of existence and presence. When the man left this second beginning it was obvious the first would be erased forever.

There would be no turning back as I have found over the last twenty years of searching out the answers that were never given to me despite my nether ending asking. Time always moves in a foreword direction that we cannot stop and reverse no matter how very strong the wish.

Maksim was a book that was forever locked and would never, up to the books demise be opened and read.

How I have so very wished all these years that the answers to my humble questions had been answered in his life rather than to trawl through the maybes after his death. So much easier but I guess ease is often out of our reach and to find the whole truth we have to look closely and eliminate the fiction from the fact.

Who are you I would ask constantly over a breakfast of fresh eggs and toasted bread. The answer would always be the same – Simply, Max. Max that had a life that was a closed chapter in a book that would never be read. A book that had neither beginning nor centre, only the conclusion that was for the reader to peruse.

His life was a guarded secret at all times. The key had been turned and discarded forever, maybe only ever once to be turned again in the final moments of my own exhausting search years later.

Occasionally, very occasionally he would let his shield slip momentarily and offer a slight glimpse into the man that he had been and allow only the shortest of gazes into his memory. These short, unguarded lapses were usually over the table at meal times and would be retracted as quickly as they had been offered.

On one occasion I recall that he spoke about his early childhood and that he had continued to be breastfed until he was seven years old. He recalled, with the slightest of smiles that his mother would hide away from him as he searched for her to be fed, the hungry child eager for the breast milk from the mother who had grown weary in the passing of years and could yield no more.

On another occasion he spoke of a childhood memory with a brother, older than himself. How they would make cigarettes out of dried corn husks and hide away out of view to smoke these in the trees that surrounded the village.

Another occasion he seemed happy to recall was again spending teenage years with the brother and how they would steal Slivovitz from the family home and hide in the nearby woods and get hopelessly drunk (Slivovitz is a distilled beverage made from damson plums. It is frequently called plum brandy and is part of the category of drinks called Rakia).

The darkest of memories that he briefly offered is of the night his world had been changed forever. He spoke of a night that attacking troops had led the occupying forces to the houses where he and his family lived. He recalled that whilst the occupying troops surrounded the dwellings the militia men had shot and beaten to death everyone they came across without mercy. With great sadness he recalled that he had seen his own son being tethered and then cut to death by the laughing invaders. This is the very last memory he offered for the rest of his life to the other half of himself that had been born, raised and loved in those foreign parts, now so distant.

What I always found strange in these short and rare glimpses into his memories was that he would never speak of names. Even when prompted for names of the people he fondly spoke about he would instantly switch and speak of other things never to be persuaded back to the earlier conversation.

My parents recall that they would intentionally ply him with his beloved whiskey in attempts at dropping his guard. Whatever the reason for his secrecy proved to be too strong a guarded secret and he always knew and would disappear to bed when he realised that his guard was slipping in the mists of drunkenness.

Whatever horrors that were lurking underneath the surface of grandfather's memory sometimes found their way to the surface in sleep. Mother recalls that as a child she would be woken in the small hours by the sounds of screams as he relived what he had experienced whilst in deep slumber.

Mother also recalls that she would forever ask two of

grandfather's closest friends, both displaced from the former Yugoslavia, about anything that would give a clue to the mystery. Again this too proved to be fruitless as if there was a code of silence that had to be adhered to. The answer she recalls would always be the same "ask Max, if he wants you to know then he will tell you."

Looking back my recollections are always of a fiercely independent man who never asked for nothing. He seemed to have never been able to fully adjust to his surroundings and the English way of life.

He would do things either by his way or no ones way. At times I fear that he would continue with things that he had started regardless of whether he thought they were truly right or not. If he thought at the beginning that he was right then right he would have to be until the end, whether the final outcome was positive or negative. He would never admit that, yes perhaps he had been wrong after all.

Every project he undertook, either it was work within the house or constructing something on the allotment was painstakingly carried out by hand. I can never recall ever seeing him use a power tool of any description, despite these being readily available at a reasonable cost.

Probably the most memorable feat of construction I remember was the well he had dug to access the water table on the allotment. This always amazed me both as a child and to the last time I saw it some five years ago.

It was maybe thirty feet in depth and perhaps just over two feet in diameter. Its construction was square and was impeccably lined the whole of its depth by brickwork.

If at any time I hear mention of a well I am always taken back to the summer of 1977. This summer was particularly a hot one and goes down on record as such. Britain was in the grip of drought and water was in ration with communal taps being installed rather than the water supply being fed to individual houses across many of our towns and cities.

Like most young kids in my area I was the proud owner of

an ancient air rifle and would spend hours on the allotment shooting at anything from rusty tin cans to targets drawn on the boundary fences and would idle away the long summer holidays from school losing myself in thought that I was master sharpshooter of all time.

One day during the long august holiday of that year was particularly hot, too hot for the usual games of cricket and soccer that would occupy the days of us

bored teenagers away from school.

After watching the repeated offers that made up children's television I decided that the order of the day would have to be the allotment with its solace and more importantly gentle, cooling breeze and long shadows which offered at least some respite from the ever gazing sun.

Armed with rifle in hand, lead pellets as ammunition and four pints of water from the newly installed emergency communal tap I set of on the days forage and adventure. The journey passed uneventful but this was not unusual as the allotment was situated a mere twenty metres form my parents house.

As usual upon reaching my destination I found that the old paneled door to my chosen hunting ground was unlocked, granddad would, I guessed have been here already as soon as the sun gave enough light for him to see.

As I made my way into the oases of lush vegetable patches it amazed me how so much life there was here amidst the scorched surrounding vegetation that had succumbed to dehydration.

Despite my calling and walking the entire breadth of the enclosed allotment granddad was nowhere to be seen. A stroke of luck perhaps on my part today as the obligatory tin can may not be the only chosen target in his absence I thought as I eyed a passing starling that perched itself, preening its iridescent plumage as it landed on a nearby fence. The willful killing of any bird in the allotment was totally outrageous in granddads eyes and would be met with rage. He saw them as the gardener's friend, an ally to help in the combat of the myriads of tiny creatures that invaded his space and dared to take microscopic size bites out of his cherished cabbages. What eyes do not see, eyes will not know as I gently raised the air rifle in the direction of the unaware target, still busily tending its feathers and enjoying the morning sunshine. Slowly now, ever so slowly the rifles sights steadied on the poor, unsuspecting feathered friend of the gardener. With forefinger trembling I began to squeeze down on the trigger......"Help, help me" came the eerie voice from beneath my feet. I recall being so shaken by this unsuspecting sound that I dropped the rifle to the ground, forcing the trigger mechanism to operate sending the lead projectile skywards into nowhere.

I looked around; everything was as it should be. I was alone but quite sure I had heard a distinctive voice calling for help. Maybe memories distort over the passing of time but if you were to ask me now I would swear it was the poor starling, in what could have been its final moment, asking to be spared.

Steadying myself and regaining the composure of a brave sharpshooter I picked up the discarded rifle and reloaded it with another lead pellet scanning for my next precision shot. All was quiet and no feathered foe were in my eager sight so I proceeded further into the allotment, stealth was the key in my quest for action so progress was cautious and slow......"Oh help me someone" came the voice but this time it appeared to come from the ground all around me. Although the words were recognizable I recall thinking that it sounded like that of Hollywood spirits, a mixture between voice and breeze, as if its very essence was in the warm subtle wind that drifted slowly all around.

This time there was no mistaking, this was a voice that sounded so very distant but so very near. Not from one direction as if someone calling but from everywhere. Ghost I remember thinking as I turned and ran as fast as my legs could carry me. Not just a ghost but the devil himself I thought as I stood gasping for breathe once outside the now forbidding confines of the imposing allotment.

Slowly the sharpshooters pride returned once more but,

fearing the essence of the days adventure had been lost, or rather scared from me I returned the thirty or forty steps home, hung my rifle to rest and, like all trepid adventurers, asked mam what time dinner would be ready.

Thankfully the rest of the day was uneventful, no visitations from long dead spirits crept from the depths of time and it's possible that the afternoon's television was not too fraught with repeated films.

I recall it being around 7pm when Nana made the journey from her side of the street to ours to enquire if anyone had seen Max. Apparently he had left as usual at daybreak for the allotment and had not returned, not even for his beloved Teachers Whiskey which was his very lifeblood back then. No one had seen him at all throughout the day, and, after another trip to the allotment it was decided that he was well and truly missing.

After telephoning the Police we sat I recall and discussed the scenarios. Only one thing was possible, he'd had a jackpot win on his beloved horse racing and was blind drunk somewhere.

Back then a telephone to the local constabulary usually meant that an officer would attend within reasonable time and, true to form there soon came the obligatory "Policeman's" knock at the door. "Hello, hello, hello" would be from memory of police response but I cannot remember the words. After a brief discussion the search began on the still unlocked allotment. Within minutes the ghostly voice resound throughout the air, again communicating the same appeal of "help me". Maybe the Police Officer was not a believer in the never world for he continued with his search uninterrupted, like a detective sleuth on the trail of a jewel thief. No sooner had the search started then it was over. Standing over the exposed well the officer called us over and, with the aid of his flashlight, revealed a rather disheveled granddad, maybe ten feet below, wedged tight against the brickwork.

After much heaving with the aid of an old, oily length of rope granddad was hoisted to safety. Battered and bruised from his ordeal he explained that the well had been dry and he suspected that this may be down to a blockage and had climbed down to investigate. He had lost his footing and fell, only to come to a stop when he became wedged tight.

I recalled the ghostly voices from earlier and the penny dropped. That is why the noise seemed to come from everywhere. It was being transmitted through the empty underground waterway and surfaced everywhere that the ground offered its escape.

And then You Find, Ten Years Have Got Behind You.....

As teenage years beckoned the magnetic bond that held us so close seemed to strengthen and I found myself wanting so desperate to discover the true man that had played such a significant part in my early years.

The tide was slowly turning and I now found myself wanting to draw back the veil around the man rather than just be drawn to the fascination that surrounded him because he was so different.

With the slow passing of time came the acquired knowledge that I gleamed from spending time browsing the pitiful array of books in the local libraries. Anything that had the merest of information of Yugoslavia would be taken home and read.

The information was scant to say the least and probably quite antiquated in its content. This was during the dawn of the package holiday when the ardent traveler would relish the dream of exotic places like France and Spain. Yugoslavia to the majority was still far beyond the realms of perception for all but the intrepid and devout explorers of a world unknown to which we were not accustomed.

Foreign language lessons at school were becoming commonplace and focused on mostly French, Spanish and German. Maybe if we were meant to travel to such extreme places as the out of reach Balkans then these languages surely would have been placed within our reach during the most precious years of our education.

Slowly, ever so slowly I was arming myself with the desperate information that I sought. Yugoslavia I read was a beautiful place of mountains forests and mystery. Through the very basics of the information that the feeble books offered and the aura that followed granddad around I always seemed to connect with a place I had never seen. They say that some people have the gift to somehow feel the background image of someone through only there presence. Maybe this is true in all of us for I could always sense distant images of places so alien to me whenever I was in his presence.

Like most kids I was interested in war games and battles of old. Unlike most kids however I had always been the odd soldier in the streets of Featherstone. Whenever the great battles had been replayed and, before the first make believe shot had been fired, sides were drawn. These were fairly simple to decide, always victorious British commando or the ever defeated German storm trooper. Not so easy whenever I was drawn into the conflict of warfare. "What side" I recall they would ask, "Us or them?" My reply would always be the same – "Yugoslavia". As usual I would be left to my own devices and, given no support in the ensuing battle would simply fight my own guerrilla war against everyone. Looking back it still surprises me how many actual battles young Yugoslavia was victorious in given the fact that I was one against many.

Although I do not recall any specific influence that I may have been directly exposed to it is easy to see that granddad had indeed ingrained his beliefs and feelings into me as a child. By the time that I was in the latter stages of teenage years I understood and believed, most importantly, believed, that Granddad had been served such a great injustice, that what he had so loyally fought for had been swept away so cruelly and should be rectified at all costs.

He was always fragmented in his answer to any question but I would scurry away and obtain information from his reply.

I accumulated from the very fragments of information that he offered that he had fought, during world war two and had suffered very harsh conditions, living from day to day in the vast mountain ranges that made up the then Yugoslavia.

Prior to his involvement in the armed struggle for liberation of his fatherland he once, only once spoke of the night that enemy troops entered his village and, without any show of mercy butchered man, woman and child and raised the buildings to the ground.

That he had to witness the brutal slaying of his own son in the hands of crazed, knife slashing madmen and, in one night, his very world was blown apart, never to be pieced together again.

I recall too that he despised bitterly the war time British Prime Minister, Winston Churchill and would fly into a rage whenever he was shown on television. Again he never gave reason for this only that Churchill had been responsible for the death of so many of his people.

With later reading I have found that Winston Churchill, a staunch one time supporter of the Yugoslav people had switched his allegiance overnight to that of Josip Broz's (Tito) communist partisans and had sealed the fate for thousands of fighters in Yugoslavia. A fate that would inevitably end, like their leader, in death. That's why; I found years later, the hatred and bitterness whenever he was shown on television.

It is sad that a man can live his life without having any past, a past that he can share amongst people he loved so deeply. Life is built on memories and without being able to pass on memories of ones life this must have been so painful without relief.

The only past he had for the world was locked away in himself and those of his own kind who had suffered the same fate. The slightest glimpse of this past could be found in an old suitcase he kept locked upstairs in the house. Looking into the suitcase was deeply forbidden and would be met with anger if ever he found that it had been opened.

Despite the danger I would often creep, peek for a moment. Within these confines was the man. I remember letters, their hand in some strange language unknown to me. Photographs of people never known and passports.

I will always remember that. Why should one man have so many passports?

The case was a closed book, like Maksim. Whenever the lid was closed so was the man.

I recall, in sadness, opening the case for the very last time, after his death. It was so empty like his memories. Most of the contents had been removed as if he knew his dying fate and was brushing over his footprints in time forever.

Remaining within the confines of the old case were photographs of women and children, writing on the back of these in Serbian, a collection of resettlement papers and a brass military emblem which appeared to be a military cap badge and two, gold and mother of pearl uniform buttons.

Only one of these photographs had ever been shown to me by granddad. I remember having coffee there when he came into the living room and put the photograph on the table and tapped it with his finger. "Which one am I"? He asked as he glanced at me with a wry smile. The photograph was that of a group of uniformed men, some sitting, others were standing and one lying down at the forefront. The person lying down was in military uniform and the brass military badge in my possession could be clearly seen upon his cap. I recall the smile as he pointed at this figure and simply said "Maksim". No sooner had the photograph appeared than it was picked up and taken back upstairs to the safety of its protective suitcase.

Intrigued by this strange act with the photograph I attempted to coax him into conversation about his exploits during world war two. I remember asking him what rank he had held, I started with corporal and he motioned his hand as if to say higher, sergeant I asked, again the hand motioned higher but this time he laughed, turned and left the room. The conversation was gone forever.

The next time I was to see the photograph would be five or six years later following his death. Strangely it had been defaced. Individual's faces had been erased by scratching away at the paper as if vital clues were removed forever.

Chapter Three –
Re - Tossing the Coin
Maksim Ćulumović (Ćulum) 1909 – 1988

Till Death Us Do Part

NANA PASSED AWAY IN **1987** after suffering the cruel effects of senile dementia for the previous three years. Dementia is a terrible thing to happen to someone. I recall that she gradually regressed from woman to child prior to her death and towards the end was solely dependant on those around her, especially granddad whose life had become that of carer, nurse and almost parent to the woman he had loved.

The illness finally took its toll whilst she was in hospital after suffering a broken leg. This was the final straw that her ravaged body could not handle and she sadly passed away oblivious to the loved ones around her.

I remember going straight to granddad after she had died and how he had cried as I placed my arms around him. I had never seen the man cry before and this hurt me so much.

I would visit him everyday to keep him company, walking

the couple of miles from the house that I had bought following the birth of my daughter Sasha.

Within months of Nana's passing he began complaining of pains in his back. This was totally out of character as I had never known him complain of having any illness. Even when it had been obvious that he was unwell he would not say. He started to eat very little, and, when he did was violently sick.

Eventually he was persuaded to seek medical advice and was referred to the local hospital. X rays confirmed that he had an abnormality showing on one lung. Further tests using a camera inserted down his throat diagnosed that he had a cancerous growth on his stomach and that it was terminal and that nothing could be done.

In that one word my entire world was blown apart. Terminal, the end. I remember walking, just walking in no particular direction nor heading for no particular destination. They say that it is a very fine rope that we walk between sanity and insanity and one wrong step could be the difference. Looking back I now see that I had in fact taken that wrong step and was spiralling into mental breakdown.

I convinced myself that everyone was wrong and that I was right. The man would never die and was immortal. He was untouchable and would always be there for me, he was the closest friend that I would ever have and, most of all, he was so very different and unique, unlike anyone else that I had known. He was the foreign soldier that I became when playing out fantasies of past battles in the streets as a child.

At night I would get hopelessly drunk and in the early hours leave the house and walk to nowhere, lost in my own intoxicated thought.

It was July and the Drs had said that he had a matter of months to live, that he would not last until Christmas. Cancer is the cruellest of diseases and I watched hopelessly as it quickly took its toll. The giant was dwindling before my very eyes; the brightest of gazes was flickering like that of a candle that had burned through the night.

Those months remain a blur, a lost segment in my life. I

would visit him religiously daily either at his home or during periods he spent in hospital. Christmas approached and mother wanted him home to spend what would be his last Christmas with the people he loved round him, in surroundings that he knew.

That Christmas day will stay heavily ingrained in my memory for the rest of my life. I remember every minute detail as if it was today. From what we ate to the clothes that people wore.

With Christmas gone his condition quickly worsened and he became bedridden. With little choice he was admitted to Ackton Hospital on the fringes of Featherstone. It was whilst here that the cancer took its cruellest turn. It spread to his brain and at times he would act out his previous life in Yugoslavia. He would relive his time spent fighting in the mountains and would speak of leading men through Bosnia to the safety of the allies in liberated Italy. He would rarely speak English and we would take his close friend with us on visits as an interpreter.

At times he would fly into wild rages and I remember being so frightened whenever he went into a rage because I had never seen the man angry before. He would sit upright in bed, startled from sleep and draw his finger across his throat in gestured threat whilst shouting orders to unseen fighters.

His condition worsened and he was placed into a single room away from the main ward. He barely woke from his morphine induced slumber and on the morning of March 17th 1988 his final fight for freedom came to an end and he quietly passed away.

To this day, as I write I will never forget the utter feeling of desolation as my parents solemnly broke the news that Maksim had fought his very last battle and, this time it was the cruel cancer that had taken away what others had not managed to do so over forty years before.

I simply stared at their saddened faces and waited for the punch line to the joke that never materialised. There was some mistake I remember repeating over and over, refusing to accept what had always been inevitable. Maksim had gone. Maximus as I fondly saw him had fought the final gladiatorial battle in the stage of his final years and had wasted and died. He had not died the hero's death but had simply moved on piece by piece as the cancer had ravaged his body until his very soul had conceded and accepted its final fate.

The weeks that followed were a complete blur, a missing piece now of my life forever. I vaguely remember attending the sombre funeral only that the Vicar had made the event as Orthodox as he possibly could given he was Church of England.

I can still see clearly in my minds eye the grief laden sobs of mother as she read the simple card that I had embedded in the bouquet of flowers. Simply it read "To the best friend that I have ever had, and could ever have."

It was so ironic that at the cemetery I noticed for the first time that the burial plot that Nana already occupied was directly backing onto granddads closest friend whom had died prematurely some seven years prior. So close in life they would now rest head to head for eternity.

As the blurring of deep grief slowly eased a little I found the courage to enter the house, a place that was filled with so very memories and was now cold and so very empty. In every room I entered I expected him to be there, the smile to fill a thousand hearts with love to be etched upon his face in simple greeting. He was not and never would be there again I found myself thinking as I slowly took in the atmosphere of the house for the very last time, straining to take in how it looked through tear stained eyes.

Mother had told me that whatever I wanted from the house was mine to take. Materialistic things however can never be a substitute for loss and I cupped in my hands the only item that meant so much to me, a deeply engraved pocket watch that I had bought him as a gift some six years prior.

As I held the watch in the empty room I was taken back to that day. I felt the warmth that filled the room from the coal fired stove and could smell the aroma of fresh bread and lamb stew simmering away gently.

Nana was sat in her floral patterned chair nearest the glowing coals of the fire, granddad sat opposite on the sofa. "Andre" (he never pronounced the w) he said as I stepped into the room. I walked over and placed the box in front of him on the small table. "What's this?" he asked looking at the box. I remember as if it were yesterday the warm glow that spread across his face as he slowly drew the watch from its box running his fingertips over the engraved scene of a deer in woodland.

With the warmest of smiles he looked at me and cupped his huge hands over the watch and held it up near to his left cheek. I felt something warm in my own cupped hand and looked down at the same watch, the room cooled and the fire was gone. The furniture remained but I stood in the room alone, so very alone apart from the memories and grief.

Without even a final glance I turned quickly and left the room for the very last time, the watch held tightly in the hand that would be its only holder for the next twenty years.

Even today as I write the final chapter to the memories of the man that had given me so much, the mentor who had mentored the young disciple, the feelings of being cheated remain embedded in my very soul. So many questions had remained unanswered in his life and I sensed the guilt that he would have carried with him. The hopelessness that he would have felt never being able to tell his own story, and the burden of having to carry this without the relief of being able to share this burden with the loved ones around him.

How he must have sat alone at night, people all around him but feeling so very alone, an island cut off in the thoughts and memories that could never be told. Maybe it was his way of protecting those people around him or maybe his mind had simply locked away and fragmented the life of love, happiness and horror that he had known.

The Beginning of the End

With his death granddad had become a closed book. The pages of Maksim Ćulumović were sealed without the chance for anyone to peruse the pages as if the book had never existed.

The initial shock ever so gradually faded and was replaced by the desperate and consuming feeling of loneliness. Although I was surrounded by family, I felt for the first time in my life, so very alone and isolated.

The rock had now gone and I felt myself drifting into my own thoughts more and more. Birthdays and Christmas were especially poignant and I would wait for the greeting card that never came.

Regrets, I held so many in the coming months but the biggest regret would continue to haunt me to this day. Sometime in early 1984 he expressed that he should write a book. This shocked me as he had been so illusive with any information in all of the time he spent in England. I asked what the title of the book would be and he simply replied "Displaced Persons" and whatever he had to say he said would "be of interest to all that read the pages of his life".

Looking back I had been so foolish to brush this to one side without thought, given the tremendous endeavours I would pursue in the next twenty years to scratch away at the mans surface.

Unfortunately, at the time I was fighting for my own beliefs and livelihood, having being caught up, as a young coal miner, in the bitter, year long miners strike that had gripped the nation. The strike passed with countless stories being told of the political struggle. How very sad that I did not take up the challenge and tell the man's story as he had wished. Maybe then I would not have been consumed by my own inner desire to pick out the fragments of his life in order to put these into their final print.

In the summer of granddads death my parents holidayed

in the Adriatic resort of Makarska, now part of independent Croatia.

On their return they visited me and I was told that they had attempted to find the illusive village of granddads birth to at least retrieve some of his native soil to spread on his final resting place.

The good friend that had acted as interpreter had to some degree finally broke the silence and written the name of granddads birth village down on a scrap of paper.

My parents had hired a car for the day and set off trying to follow the forty year old directions he had wrote and, after maybe eight hours of driving through rugged terrain they had stumbled on a place that mother recognised from one of granddads talks to her as a child. They recall that the village appeared quite dilapidated and was approached by driving over a shallow stream lined with old timbers. One of the first buildings they encountered, and the largest, was that of a store and makeshift bar combined. They idled the car opposite to this building and showed an elderly resident the piece of paper that had the details written on of granddad and their hoped destination. The man glanced at the paper and appeared to show little interest before turning and carrying on with his chore.

Moving onwards into the small hamlet they again drew slowly to a halt to where a group of locals were idling the day with idle banter. Again they were beckoned to look at the offered piece of paper and again their response was that of disinterest and somewhat disapproval before turning to return to their conversation. Mother recalls that she felt as if there very presence in the village was being scrutinised and questioned in the fast pace of the locals banter.

One elderly gentleman however left the group and approached the car once more. He motioned to be shown the paper again and, after slowly scrutinising it he pointed towards the track that led to the last of the dwellings and then with two upturned fingers, motioned that once they reached these buildings they should walk in the pointed direction.

With the most nervous of thank you's they drove the cat the twenty or so metres to the last of the village buildings and drew the car to a gentle halt as the track slowly gave way to thick grass before being lost from sight.

Turning the ignition off they opened the car doors and were immediately met by an approaching police officer coming from the direction of the group of locals whom they had spoken with. On first impressions it was obvious that the officer was not happy, on second impressions, given that he had drawn his firearm, it was obvious that he was maybe just a little angry.

Guns and not understanding the bearers language mother recalls is quite chilling to say the least and she remembers having the feeling that she was to die hundreds of miles from home in a place she did not know, (I myself would momentarily experience the same feelings of dread, momentarily some twenty years later in my own quest for the illusive village). She recalls instinctively her arms rose above her head in instant surrender which she said thankfully appeared to calm the explosive situation and that the officer sheaved the gun in its holster.

No sooner had this happened when a car came towards them from the direction of the village and that two plain clothed men climbed from its interior and, after exchanging the briefest of acknowledgement with the officer seemed to take charge of the situation.

In between silent prayers mothers recalls pushing her memory to its limit trying to recall anything that granddad had told her that may diffuse the situation. She recalls that he would always speak to her as a child how he loved to swim and that not too far from where he had lived there had been a beautiful river and lake. Now she was faced with a problem. He would speak of Pliva and Pivo. She remembered one was a river, the other a beer.

Luckily mothers gamble paid off as she said Pliva to the interrogators as she lowered her hand to shade her eyes in the gesture of scanning the horizon. Pliva is a river in that part of Bosnia, imagine the explaining she would have to have undergone had she chose the other...."I am here looking for beer!"

Not entirely satisfied the captures gestured the motions of swimming and bathing costumes, prodding at father's clothing as if to prompt him to reveal that underneath he was indeed equipped for a marathon swim.

With no bathing costume offered the attention was directed towards the rental car and, although barriers to language were too strong, mother recalls that it was obvious that accusations were being made that maybe the car had been stolen. Maybe the three wise men had uncovered two of Europe's most evil of villains who had neither entered the village to swim in Pliva or drink Pivo but were there for underworld activities unknown to them, or, maybe not. Whatever the reasons for the harsh treatment are still not known to this day but the experience obviously shook mother badly and it would be another nineteen years until she would set foot on Yugoslav soil again.

With no evidence to further hold the two the men gestured for them to get in the hire car and to follow their own vehicle. They drove my parents out of the village and onto a road where they gave them directions south from whence they came.

On returning to England my parents wrote to the Yugoslavian Embassy in London. The reply followed within the week and the only explanation offered was that they had caused a great deal of curiosity in the area during their interrupted visit and that staff at the Embassy apologised at their mistreatment.

Whatever had been written on that piece of paper I will never know as mother, still frightened from the ordeal destroyed it immediately.

The following years saw little or no progress in my search. Letters to the Embassy in Belgrade proved fruitless with no information offered about any Maksim Ćulumović and, at times I would even question myself whether or not the man had ever existed.

What made matters even worse was the spelling of the name. As a child mother had recalled seeing the name written with two different spellings, Ćulumović and Čulumovic. Although to my own eyes the difference between the letters C having either Ć or Č was negligible I would be informed years later that this difference was a significant factor in tracing a family name and that the spelling of Čulumovic was very rare indeed. So rare that it would be highly likely that anyone with the name spelt in this particular way would be related in family.

Unfortunately catastrophic events unfolded in Yugoslavia in the early 1990's with the country plunging into civil war.

British television was filled with scenes of utter horror and carnage and has the months slowly passed a vile terror was unleashed as the conflict spread into Bosnia.

I remember being drawn to the horrific media coverage and would become emotional for reasons not known to me. Until then I had been led to believe that Maksim had been Serbian and had lived his life in Serbia. He had never once mentioned Bosnia only prior to his death when he had relived events fighting there.

I recall the feelings of hatred I felt for the people that were responsible on all sides of the conflict for their acts of murder and savagery and was deeply saddened for a country I had never visited only in my imagination. My determination to seek out the truth was being refuelled with every murderous act that was portrayed on screen and I found myself drawn even more deeply to the country and its people. A magnetic pull which would reach out and envelope me in its grasp that has its clench on me to this day.

Is There Anybody Out There?

People say that grieving is a slow progress that only time can heal. Just as you get used to losing a loved one you see their reflection, briefly either in shop windows or passing cars and, when you turn, they are again gone from you.

Maybe grief never leaves us at all and we cope with the loss rather than forget. Looking back on all the years I searched, and continue to do so, its more than probable that with every scrap of information gleaned I was keeping the man alive in my own heart and I so very felt the need to remain connected to him, to bridge the divide between life and death.

With his passing there was a great void in my own inner self and the searching for anything connected with him always felt like once again a small part of me was within his very presence after his death.

I had been given a taste, only that, of a people so different to what I was accustomed and now wanted the full meal. I would visualize a place so beautiful and serene, a place only written in books and depicted in pictures from long ago. I would dream of walking through a place of long grass, blowing gently in the cool breeze, stepping, like a child into the footprints of the man that had walked so many years before. I would hear the laughter and gaze at the child; shouting at the mother wanting to be fed from the breast so eagerly but then, as always the breeze died and the grass and the dream was again gone.

Some say the internet is a curse created my mankind, others say that it is one of the wanders of modern world. My own introduction to this powerful tool came belated and is now only in its third year.

My search was amplified with the information now available and hours each day would be spent typing in the very basic information that I had. Name, date of birth and nationality, Serbian. I had one photograph, that of a uniformed man, a brass military cap badge, two gold and mother of pearl tunic cuff buttons and a photograph of King Petar II Karađorđević.

Genealogies in the UK as become big business with everyone wanting to find their roots. Maybe we search in the hope of discovering unknown riches of millionaires that we can tap into to gain wealth or maybe its simple curiosity in which we search.

Thankfully it seems that the interest is world wide and I found a web site devoted to Serbian Genealogy. Maybe I expected too much, and received little. Despite posting for Ćulumović or Čulumovic people there came nothing in the way of information.

I would post on the forum with utter determination, each scrap of evidence would be sent with the ever hoping that someone, some where would make the connection and finally give me the answers that I so desperately searched.

Mother recalled the village of her mistreatment as being something akin to the pronunciation of Briani and again this information was posted on the websites forum. Two photographs with faint handwriting, one in the Cyrillic alphabet, the other using the Latin alphabet were carefully translated for me by readers of the forum.

The first photograph in Cryıllic depicted two woman and a teenage girl, all looking quite sombre and dressed in dark clothing had the writing; "To Maksim, reminiscing and long remembering from your wife and daughter Zorka and niece Milka, lot of respect Stojana."

The second was written in the Latin alphabet and portrayed two women, three young girls and a boy. This inscription reads; "To my son in-law Maksim Ćulumović with greetings from Liubica, Stojan, Radmila, Rade, Violeta and Budimir, 27/02/1949, Bijelo Polje, Independent State of Montenegro.

One of the women in this photograph is almost identical in appearance to the wife, Stojana in the first picture.

Although granddad had always relayed to me that his family were dead, mother recalls that as a child she would in fact help him put together packages of tea and other items, which he would send to a sister in-law that had survived. She recalls too the anger he had shown one day and her childhood memories, maybe clouded in time, recalled that the reason for this anger was that he had found that the sister in-law had married a communist. Whatever the reason she cannot recall any more communication taking place between the two.

She can also remember, as a child seeing the picture of the three women and, as children often do, she laughed at their appearance. The three were rather stern looking individuals, dressed not for the swinging 60's, but more akin to people from the desolate times of hardship following warfare. She recalls granddad hurriedly putting the picture into his pocket and scorned her severely for laughing at his wife. Mother never saw the photograph again until his death.

Armed with this information and finally a connection to a place I focused on Montenegro as my target search.

Finally I thought this was the connection I had been searching. Bijelo Polje actually existed and for the next six months all of my attention was drawn to this place. A place of beauty nestled within the sheer eye catching scenery of the country that surrounded the town.

Again hours upon hours were spent corresponding on both Serbian and Montenegrin forums with little, more to the point, no success. Ćulumović was not a native name there and, from the many people I spoke with on the forums, was unheard of in that region.

For months I held onto this flickering flame of hope that with a place my search was finally over. With every week the flame died a little more until the stark realisation came that, at least where Bijelo Polje was concerned, I would find no answers.

I would look endlessly at these photographs and imagine these people in life, trying to beckon them back into reality to answer my questions. Photographs can be so cruel. They allow us to peer at the person but never the essence of the being, the memories and knowledge, nor their stories. Without the story the image is useless and only acts as a tantalising glimpse to torture and despair when we try and read the picture without the explanation or reason.

Whenever I looked, and still do at these two photographs my mind is cast back to my own childhood and how different the life of the subjects, must have been for those portrayed to my own.

Granddad I now see was also living the life that he dreamed of during his years in England. Although to me he seemed happy with our way of life I now realise just how alienated and so alone he would have felt. He was not just being "different and stubborn" as people would often remark but was merely continuing his very self in an environment he was not accustomed and could never fully adjust, up until his death.

Maybe, just maybe that is the reason for my extensive, never ending search. To give back what the man had endeavoured passionately to install into my soul so that the story may continue.

Maybe the poor tomato boy, with the wheelbarrow was purposely engrained into me, as was the lone soldier on the battlegrounds of Featherstone; long after the fight had gone, whatever the reasons in life, the child had grown, but the lifelong dream of uncovering the truth would never be gone.

Bijelo Polje and Montenegro held whatever secrets it had within its clutches and offered no fragment of hope for me in my search. This I found was to be the first of countless frustrations that I would encounter over the coming years. For the first time I had images of real people and a real place, not just a place of possibles and maybes, but an actually place of real people.

Looking back, maybe I was not yet prepared to face the enormity of what I sought and the feeling of frustration and fading hopes would continue with every step foreword I would make, only to be stopped dead in my tracks and start over once again.

Suggestions on the Yugoslav forum suggested that my search could have links to the Lika area of Croatia as there was a place resembling mother's recollections of the pronunciation of her visit. She wrote Briani, posts to the forum suggested Brianne and that this place was laying to the west of Pliva National Park. This was finally I thought the connection without doubt. A place and a direct connection to the word

Pliva. Pliva that granddad spoke about so fondly from the days of his youth, how he would swim in the rivers and waterfalls.

Again with determination I explored every possibility of this place and months were spent scrutinising every aspect that I may be now following a course that would raise the veil finally.

As the months passed however so too did the hope. Ćulumović families had been known in the area but after correspondence none knew of the names of neither Maksim nor people depicted on the photographs. Again I was drawn to the stark possibility that the man of my search had never existed and was now becoming convinced, as I always had suspected from the beginning, that the identity had been changed and that, quite possibly my questions would never be answered.

With every set back came the memories of the man that was. I would be drawn forever back to another time in my life that I felt secure, to the very days of my own real happiness and contentment.

I would recall the warmth I felt whenever I was within the mans presence and the security that this feeling offered.

My thoughts would drift back to school years where I would call at the house to make sure that the buckets of coal were full and would last until my return from my day of schooling.

I would recall, in particular two of those days each year when there would be a crudely baked circle of bread placed on the table with a lone candle burning brightly within its centre. I would recall rushing home from school in adolescent eagerness to see if the candle still burned. As always it did, as brightly as it did on my visit earlier in the day and would continue to do so well within the night.

I would recall too the merriment and mirth that would follow in that house as evening came, of the table being so full of the most beautiful of food, cold hams, freshly baked breads, cheeses and potatoes, to remember a few.

Drink would flow throughout as if there was a never ending

supply and the older generations, fuelled by its effects would proceed to make attempts at a strange dance, their aged bodies could no longer accomplish.

As always my childish self would still be drawn to the burning bread that had retained its fire for so long and would enquire with hungry anticipation if this too could be eaten. "No" was always the disappointing reply, this was being saved for the Saints. He would say that the celebrations were his "Glory Day" but would never elaborate further. Since my search I have found that he was in fact celebrating the family Slava, a custom he continued until his death.

(Slava is the Orthodox Christian Custom of honoring a family patron saint. It is traditionally celebrated by the Serbs).

Maybe the first of the real breakthroughs came for me in the spring of 2007. For years now I had traced every step of information I had without even the glimmer of hope.

Now, for reasons still not known, mother invited me to meet with the last of the surviving Yugoslavians that had arrived in the UK following their exodus from post war Yugoslavia.

He was the young cousin to granddads friend and was now maybe in his late 70's.

Armed, like the most trepid explorer I visited him with my parents, prepared with all the information I had.

I was made; I remember, most welcome with the offer of coffee and cakes and felt comfortable in their presence and offered hospitality.

Mother had not seen the man since her early years and much of the meeting was spent on reminiscing and catch up stories to bridge the gap of familiarity.

I passed the man the patchy information that I had gleaned painstaking over the years and waited for his response.

I remember he leafed through the notes I had made and, quite strangely to my thoughts expressed his concerns that maybe I should stop the search immediately. I asked why and he simply said that the place of my search was now occupied by the Muslim faith and I would find nothing there to help me. So vividly I recall then as he turned over the photograph of the uniformed Maksim, even more vividly his response of "Chulum". Even more so I recall his wife's response as he voiced the name, she rose from her chair and, harshly corrected him, that this was not his name. He retreated immediately and shrugged that no; just the nickname he knew him as.

Little if any information was gleamed from this meeting and I came away with little more than I had set out with.

It was like encountering a code of silence that had remained in place since they had arrived in the UK and, for whatever their reasons should never be breached at all costs.

Two things came out of that encounter, Muslims and the name Chulum. The latter I would, to my detriment, ignore for the next twelve months.

I had become knowledgeable enough to realize that the Muslim faith was closely connected to Bosnia but had never imagined that this was the place that my search should focus. In fact, within the former Yugoslavia, this would have been the last place I envisioned. He was secretive yes, but not once had I heard him mention, in the slightest, any connection to Bosnia.

Bosnia Old Country of Scars

Bosnia is home to three ethnic "constituent peoples": Bosniaks, the most numerous population group of Bosnia, with Serbs in second and Croats in third. Regardless of ethnicity, a citizen of Bosnia and Herzegovina is often identified in English as a Bosnian. In Bosnia, the distinction between a Bosnian and a Herzegovinian is maintained as a regional, rather than an ethnic distinction. The country is politically decentralized and comprises two governing entities, the Federation of Bosnia and Herzegovina and Republika Srspska. Formerly one of the six federal units constituting Yugoslavia, Bosnia and Herzegovina gained its independence during the Yugoslav Wars of the 1990s. Bosnia and Herzegovina can be described as a Federal Democratic Republic that is transforming its economy into a market-oriented system, and it is a potential candidate for joining the European Union.

Over the next weeks I scanned over satellite images of Bosnia and searched online for any maps that were available.

Numerous emails were sent to the Yugoslavian Combatants organization in London requesting any information that they could offer. Each day I would open my inbox but each day the reply never came.

Out of sheer desperation I contacted a private genealogical investigator based in Montenegro and gave her the information that I had. Quickly she got to work and spoke to most, if not all Ćulumović families in Bosnia. Although the usual response was that of pleasure that interest was being shown to trace lost people the answer was always the same, none had any connection to the name Maksim in their family history.

Months of searching online photographs paid off when I discovered one photograph of Maksim. The photograph, I researched was taken near to the town of Čakac, Serbia and depicted men from the Yugoslavian army. Granddad, as in the earlier photograph was pictured laying down at the front, either he was an extremely lazy man or the placement, always in a prone position in photographs was that of seniority. This stance would continue in later photographs after he had arrived in England. Each group photograph taken shows him in exactly the same position, laying down at the foot of the group as if his image and been superimposed onto the picture.

During this time a strange thing happened. Prior to his death I recalled seeing resettlement documents that he had kept locked away in the old suitcase. I had searched the house countless times but these avoided my gaze throughout and I thought that they must have been accidentally lost over the years.

Whist searching for something unrelated to my search I opened a writing bureau where I kept all legal documents and papers of importance. My gaze was immediately drawn to a disheveled faded brown envelope that lie on the top of the collection of documents. I tipped out the envelopes contents and was shocked, to say the least to see photographs of Maksim fall out before my eyes. After the initial shock I gathered them up and spread them carefully out onto the carpet. Not only were there photographs but resettlement paperwork from Italy, Germany and the UK.

The papers were of vital importance as they gave away personal information that he had never once divulged and had kept secret to the end.

Name, date of birth and, more importantly birthplace were recorded on each document. Strangely however both marital status and place of birth differed on each document. Birthplace was recorded as being Brzani, Brdzani and Brdjani and marital status implied that he was either single or widowed.

Other recorded information offered was that he was Serbian by Nationality, was of Orthodox religion and that Parents were Jovo and Petra (mother's maiden name had been Lukić).

On one document it was stated that the birthplace, on this spelt as Brdjani was in the province of Jaljce.

Amongst the paperwork I found documents that recorded the involvement of Police in the UK. Mother had recalled that, as a child she remembered that Police Officers would visit the house on a regular basis, and that one time in particular, that they had visited unexpectedly and had almost discovered the illegal distillation of whiskey that was being produced in the cellar.

These papers were of vital significance as I had, through a close contact, had Police records checked within what was then the Aliens Department and no record ever came back with connection to the name or the address. In the departments records neither had existed within their interest or involvement. These documents proved otherwise however, they recorded weekly dates of the visits, signatures of the attending officers and fingerprints of the man that they were monitoring.

I was drawn to the photographs amongst the collection of paperwork. Photographs of the man I had never known. A man in his youth and prime. A prime that had been taken away and would never be returned.

One in particular depicted him in full body plaster cast following the accident that had broken his back soon after he had commenced work underground at Fryston Colliery. Despite the pain and discomfort the smile shines through, the smile that would warm its way through my childhood worries and woes.

Whenever I look at this particular photograph I am instantly transported to times past. Times of sunshine and the song of birds in the hedgerows of the allotment.

He would be stood, naked to the waist and I would be drawn to the vivid scar that ran upwards along his spine. No matter how the sun darkened his skin, this would always be the whitest of white.

We would sit, wherever the shade offered and he would talk. He would talk of nature and its wonders, how the land, if respected would give back its own respect with the fruits of its offerings and we should need nothing else in life.

He would lose himself, at times in this talk and I would wait with patience for the dam of silence to break. It never would and he would withdraw momentarily into himself as if to gain composure whenever he felt that the talk was becoming too close. He would break the connection and send me to the well for water and, on my return the conversation would always be diverted as if the first had never taken place.

As always the sun would diminish too quickly and the birdsong would fade as if it never had chorused, the aromas would withdraw and I would be sat alone, as always, photograph in hand.

Maybe as I look back, true displacement is that of never ever knowing. Displacement in Maksim's case would have been seeing both sides of the coin as it was flipped. Being able to compare the sides. Both sides would have their own memories to compare, the good, the bad and the horror.

Maybe it is worse to have only ever seen one side, knowing that the other existed but could never be seen. The other face was always there but always out of sight and could never be turned.

Armed with this new information I concentrated my search on the sketchy maps available online and posted new requests for help on the Serbian forum. It was deducted that the spelling of birthplace would likely to be Brdjani or rather Brđani to be precise.

The way foreword should have been wide open for me now but, like everything else I had, and would continue to have, this was not to be the case. Brdjani or Brđani, were in abundance. I found there to be at least four places with this name in Serbia, three in Bosnia and one in Croatia.

Again weeks of frustration followed as I carefully pieced together what I had.

Jajce looked promising for my immediate search as this name was in fact a town and municipality in Bosnia and was unique. What's more there was a Brdjani / Brđani settlement lying about thirty miles south west to the town.

Numerous postings on forums proved fruitless and no information over a further period of months offered any information regarding this place.

Innocently I posted requests for help on a Bosnian forum giving the link to a blog that I had been running and posting new information relating to my search and photographs of people that, at one time had been close to granddad.

I was shocked and saddened to experience the response that my simple requests evoked.

In the safety of our armchairs we never fully take on board the news images that are filtered through to us from areas of the world that are in conflict. We see only what the authorities design for our viewing. The images are carefully constructed and staged in a manner that is carefully rehearsed never to give us the true picture of what is really happening. When new news breaks to the surface, yesterdays stories are pushed to the back of our minds and, we take on the wrong assumption that everything is now settled and the old footage of horror have been replaced with that of peace and love.

This was my first encounter during the whole of my search that everything was not settled in Bosnia. That age old beliefs and divisions were still high on the agenda and that suspicion of answering any questioning was now to block my search. People simply did not wish to speak or offer any information for fear that remembrance would evoke the sparks of division that had been there for countless years, and so remain to this day.

Within days I came to the conclusion that the forums would not offer me the magical answers that I desperately sought and that I would have to proceed again on my own without the help that I so desperately needed from the people that could have possibly held the golden key to the lock that I so agonizingly wanted to open in order that the story of my mentor could finally be read.

I had the name, Maksim Ćulumović, born on 17/11/1909 in Brdjani / Brđani in the Province of Jajce, parents were Jovo and Petra and that he had been an Orthodox Serb.

With very little choice I now faced the stark reality. It was obvious that despite my painstaking efforts maybe this would be as far as my search would take me and that if I were to proceed any further then I would have to visit Bosnia and eliminate any possibles and maybes until my goal of discovery had been reached.

People would often say to me why the need to search for something that was long gone and could never be returned. My simple answer would be that I simply desired so strongly to walk the mans footsteps, see the surroundings that he had enjoyed around him and feel the very essence of his natural surroundings just as he had done so with my own.

Looking back I now know that this desire was to be only

the tip of what I searched for so passionately, that at times I would almost be pushed by something not seen, only felt, to seek out much more than a simple patch of soil that had been trodden over many years before.

Chapter Four – In the Corner of Some Foreign Field

I HAD SWORN FOR YEARS that I would never again take to the skies and fly. For over twenty years I had become an avid believer in the saying that if god had wanted us to take to the skies then he would have created us bearing wings and not legs.

Now I was faced with the stark reality that unless I disputed my own fears of leaving solid ground then it would be highly unlikely that I would ever find whatever it was that I searched.

I discussed the possibility of visiting Bosnia with my parents and recall mother's attempts at dissuading me from travel. It appeared that the memories from her own ordeal and treatment there twenty years prior were still deeply engrained and had become even more entrenched with the atrocities that had taken place in the civil war of the 1990's.

Whatever her reasons it was clear that I should not expect any support nor encouragement from her whilst I was making my feeble attempts at planning any trip to Bosnia.

Once again I felt like the intrepid explorer who had set out on that day so long ago when Granddad had become hopelessly lodged in his well. Never straying far from home, but with thoughts so distant. I pondered for weeks over the alien world of foreign travel and online booking and made little progress in what would become the next step in my search.

Strangely then and with reasons unknown to me given the previous refusal of help, mother announced that the trip had been organised and that my parents would travel with me. The three of us would fly to Split on the Croatian coast and would spend seven days in an apartment in the resort of Makarska from when they had voyaged on that fateful day twenty years prior.

During the week stay we would hire a car and travel into Bosnia to seek out once again the elusive birthplace and, in an ideal world, the search would be over. Answers finally answered and the never knowing to be known at last.

We were to fly on September 1st 2007 which left only weeks to finalise and scrutinise the information that I had. I was convinced now that the Brdjani / Brđani that I focused was the correct place of my search and planned routes that we would travel from Makarska.

The contact from Zagreb, Croatia, that I had met online and who had helped me so much in my search (and who would eventually piece together the last fittings of the puzzle), translated into Bosnian questions that I was to ask people when I reached the area and I scanned and copied photographs that I hoped to show people when I at last reached the final destination of my quest.

The day came quickly and the journey that I held so many expectations for was underway.

Thankfully the flight from Manchester airport to Split was uneventful and we touched down safely. The final fifteen minutes of the flight will perhaps stay with me forever. The sheer beauty of the Adriatic coastline is truly breathtaking and I remained transfixed to the airplanes window until our final approach.

Outside the airport we were directed to a minibus and

within ten minutes we were being driven along the winding coastal road towards Makarska.

Gazing through the windows of the minibus I was drawn to the plots of land that seemed to fill every space that was occupied. Their uniformity and neatness mirrored that of the allotment of my memories and it seemed that even their layout was similar in its form.

As I looked in wander I realised that I was finally here. The place so instilled into my heart was now within my gaze. I struggled throughout the journey to control my inner emotions and fought so desperately to fight back the tears. The tears that had been suppressed for so many years were now finally breaching the surface and, with embarrassment in case I drew attention, feigned sleep for the rest of the journey south.

Makarska surprised me. It was not the place that I had imagined. A place of a lifestyle so idyllic and slow paced. Instead I was met with a modern holiday resort of bustling boutiques and restaurants. Newly built apartments engulfed the old quarters and spread as far as the eye could see in both directions, following the path of its shingle beaches.

Despite its apparent modern feel it was overshadowed by the impressive back drop of the Buckova mountains which forged an impenetrable wall and appeared to be pushing the town into the sea. This solid wall of stone would be magnificent at dusk and would eerily glow golden brown as the sun slipped its quiet path into the still Adriatic Sea.

The next couples of days were uneventful. I was merely a tourist in a foreign land and would slip into the routine of walking along the boutiques that lined the sea front, visit the market in the old town and then mid afternoon would meet with my parents, have something to eat and drink and return to the apartment. The rest of the evening would be spent on the balcony taking in the beauty of the views overlooking the coastline.

7am on the Wednesday we left Makarska in the hired car

that we had collected the previous evening. Prior to leaving, my father and I had engaged in a debate over currency. He was adamant that when we entered Bosnia the Euro would be honoured, I was not and said that I should exchange money into Bosnian Markas before we left Croatia.

Looking back I was foolish to succumb to his emphasis that he travelled the world on a regular basis and knew everything I did not about world travel and we left with only Croatian Kuna's and the all important Euro.

We drove along the coastline northwards and rose rapidly over the mountain range that had dominated the skyline from Makarska. The ground levelled and I was amazed at the sheer beauty before my eyes. For miles the countryside was a series of rolling hills that were met with mountain ranges, so distant on all sides.

Within thirty minutes of our departure we were stopped at a border crossing. The four uniformed men reminded those that you would see in a Hollywood movie of such a place. Uniformed, but slightly unkempt with the air of danger about them. It was obvious that they were curious but after checking paperwork they waved us through.

As we moved foreword the realisation finally hit me. I was in Bosnia at last. This was the place I had searched for so long without ever realising. In every piece of the landscape before me now I could feel the reason behind my ever searching. As we travelled further into this land my inner feelings grew stronger and I could feel his presence within me, the driving force that had taken me this far was now surfacing in this strange land.

Everything I now saw reminded me of the man that I searched. I knew that for the first time I was on the right path to uncover what I needed to quash my inner hunger, the need to know.

As we drove northwards it soon became obvious the terrible hardships and horrors that the country had suffered in the 1990's. Grave markers littered the landscape in hurriedly put together cemeteries which seemed to occupy every available pieces of space.

Small hamlets we passed were devoid of human life, their decaying buildings displaying the brunt of madness and war. Their scorched walls were pock marked with the scars of artillery and small arms fire. I could never imagine the despair and cruelty that had taken place within the confines of the now sad and broken buildings. The feelings of horror and the disbelief that must have been felt when the inhabitants succumbed to the fact that the rest of the world had simply turned their backs on them conveniently for so long.

Even the occasional buildings that remained occupied displayed their own scars of battle with most having their exteriors riddled with the wounds of gunfire.

The journey up through central Bosnia passed without problem and I amazed myself with my navigating skills in a foreign country with road signs that were unreadable. Just as I thought things would pass without problem, the first stumbling block was encountered. Strangely the manageable road signs switched from the Latin alphabet to that of the Cyrillic one. I now know that this was the invisible crossing border which separated the Croatian / Muslim Federation from the Serbian dominated Republika Srspska.

To make matters worse the weather was closing in and within thirty minutes daylight would be plunged into darkness as we were caught up in a fierce thunderstorm, the likes of which I have never experienced before. The torrential cascade of rainfall would make progress slow on the mountainous roads and it was not long before I feared that we were hopelessly lost.

By chance we happened to drive past an isolated farmhouse jus as an elderly couple were stepping outside the rough wooden door. Eagerly we pulled over and I walked towards them greeting with the customary "dobra jutro" – good afternoon just to sound impressive. Impress them I must have because their reply was in high speed Bosnian of which I had no idea. I glanced in intrigue at the elderly couple as we exchanged words none of us could understand. They were picture postcard images of what you would expect from rural Bosnia. Their clothes and even shoes were primitive and hand fashioned. I showed the elderly man the writing I had prepared and I handed him the paper his gaze caught my own.

Looking into those eyes sent me crashing through time and I felt myself looking into the eyes of the man that I searched.

It was always the eyes that betrayed the true life of the man as it does with us all. They say the eyes are the window into the soul. One moment they would be the large, proud eyes of a man that could rise above everything by using the power of his mind. The next they would become sharp and narrow. Like that of a wild, untamed animal with no discrimination or mercy. And then there were the laughing eyes of a kind and warm hearted, generous man with a carefree beauty that would capture your attention. Twelve months later I would learn that the surviving brother who had remained in Bosnia would have the same gaze of natural charm that would hold the onlooker transfixed as if being slowly but surely scrutinised.

With finger pointing as he traced the words written in the piece of paper he repeated the word Šipovo and smiled as he pointed down the road to the direction that we were travelling. The woman, smiling opened the rough door that was the entrance to their humble home and gestured me in. Without wanting to appear ignorant I stepped inside behind her and her husband and was immediately handed a tiny shot glass of slivovitz. The liquid burnt my throat and I could see the amusement on the couples faces as I coughed. The woman eagerly offered more of the fiery brandy but I offered my excuses the best I could and thanked them for the hospitality shown to me and headed back to the waiting car. With one final look back and a wave of farewell we headed onwards along the tree lined road in the pouring rain.

As we drove onwards I took in the full beauty of the landscape around me. Maybe it was the tiny shot of slivovitz that was racing through my bloodstream, like some hallucogenic drug, or maybe the land around me was simply engulfing me in its sheer beauty. Pine forests on both sides of the beaten road gave way to rugged outcrops of rock and we found ourselves dropping gently down whilst the rocky outcrops rose above us in steep, impenetrable walls of stone. It gave the illusion that at some point in time a great engineer had striven to forge the road deep into the mountain side cutting through all in his path. Maybe the real reason was simply that modern man had followed an ancient trail through this magnificent landscape and had laid down the foundations of a road in its path.

Even the oppressive weather added to the beauty that was being set out before my eyes, adding to the mystery of the place that I had searched for so long.

The road was deserted of other vehicles but occasionally we would pass lone figures walking by its side. Like the old couple they were dressed in simple clothes and appeared as if they were lost in time, taking a stroll to nowhere in the pouring rain and in no great hurry to get to their remote destination.

Eventually the road levelled and, turning sharply to the left I saw Pliva River for the first time. Like the land around me the sight of this stretch of water was breathtaking. For months prior to my journey I had searched to the point of exhaustion for this place. Above nothing else he would speak of Pliva and swimming. I would scan for hours online for any mention of Pliva and the connection I so desperately sought. Looking at the rivers, green, slow flowing waters I was shaken by the stark realisation that I was here, so close to the reality that I was to walk the footsteps of my dream. In those very waters I could almost touch the soul and spirit of what I so desperately sought. I could feel the strength and power that the green forbidding waters omitted and was drawn to the calling of a past that had almost been forgotten forever.

The road cut through a sheer landscape of beauty as it wound itself upstream, the green flow of Pliva to our right. Although the already dismal weather worsened still my spirits were at fever pitch as I knew that the town of Šipovo lay within a few miles upstream and, more importantly the hamlet of Brdjani / Brđani was within a twenty minute drive from the town.

Occasionally now we would be met with oncoming traffic which was a clear indicator that we were approaching an inhabited place. At first it shocked me at how badly the Bosnians drove as more and more of the oncoming traffic seemed to wander across the road into our path, forcing our car to swerve erratically to avoid collision. Then I began to remember the old couple's hospitality and the fiery brandy they had offered so early in the day and assumed that maybe people here drank this before taking to the road. As the instances of being forced off the road increased the dreadful truth slowly dawned on me. We had hired the car in Croatia. I remember looking it over before our journey and had pondered over the red chequered flag on the registration plate. The flag of Croatia was greeting oncoming travellers and, given the hatred still felt between Serb and Croat, this must have been a flashback to horrors unleashed in those dreadful years of the 1990's. The straying of the oncoming vehicles was not accidental I calculated, but rather a desire to see us in a burnt out heap at the roadside!

Not wishing to worry my parents I did not express my concerns and we carried on, with only me aware of the possible danger that we were facing.

Following the winding course of Pliva we entered the town of Šipovo. The heavy rain continued as we drove into the town and the only people visible were a group of teenagers who jeered as we drove past.

It was at this point that I realised that we were hopelessly lost as we encountered the first road junction. None of the signs were eligible in the native Cyrillic lettering and we drove through the town with heavy hearts and the air of disappointment filled the cars interior.

We pulled into the first petrol station we came upon. We now had less than half a tank of petrol and this would be a good place to seek out directions. Even before the car had fully come to a halt the attendant dashed out from the confines of the small shop and stood, in the pouring rain, banging on the drivers side window. Maybe he just wanted a fast sale in the torrential weather, or maybe, like the oncoming traffic he had been infuriated with the chequered flag embellished on the cars registration plate.

Whatever the reason I quickly got out of the car and stood facing him in the drenching rain. His anger was evident in the fast flowing, words that he spat at me. My own, innocent reply was simply, "Hello, how are you?" With these simple words his arms lowered and the grimace that engulfed his face subsided slowly into a smile. The upraised arms encircled my shoulders and he held me tight as he laughed. My own laugh came forth and we stood, in the rain, holding each other and laughing like two crazy men realising for the first time the punch line to a joke long since told.

With renewed confidence that I was not to be the victim of a vicious roadside assault I offered my new found friend the paper with the translated questions and, like the elderly man before he carefully scrutinised the writing, tracing it with his finger.

It was obvious that there was something on the paper that interested him as he pointed to some of the words and then in the direction that we had travelled from whilst speaking quickly. I looked and could only shrug my shoulders as he repeated words and pointed excitedly. Although both parties were equally enthusiastic to get their message across it soon became evident in the drenching rain that both were chasing a losing battle and shrugged their shoulders in unison.

Remembering that we were running low on fuel I pointed to the cars fuel cap and held out both Croatian Kuna and Euro currency. The shrugged shoulders and outstretched arms appeared again and I could understand "No Kuna, no Euro – Marka". It was obvious that the only currency that would be accepted here was the Bosnian Marka, a currency that bad planning and misplaced advice had me travelling without.

With a strong grip of the hand and heavy pat on the back we said our farewells and I clambered, down hearted, back into the car. The realisation slowly sank in that I was so close to what I desired but was still yet so far away as we headed back in the direction that we had travelled.

With heavy heart I succumbed to the realisation that I would not walk the soil that I so desperately searched and that the whole journey had simply been wasted. The one chance that I had of finally reaching my goal and possibly unveiling the secrets that it held had slipped from my weary grasp just as I thought I was to hold it in my reach.

We left Šipovo, the dark oppressive gloom of its weather exaggerated by my own inner disappointment.

Although the road signs offered no hint of our direction I knew that if we followed the path of the winding River Pliva this would take us north to the town of Jajce. Although this course would be taking us further from the Croatian border to the south, it would lead us into the Federation of Bosnia where the road signs would be in the Latin alphabet and I could then plot a course back into Makarska.

Within thirty minutes we had entered the deserted streets of Jajce and could momentarily make out in the skyline its castle, blurred by dense cloud and rainfall but remaining imposing regardless of nature's camouflage.

The famous waterfall eluded us and we drove on south. Sheer slopes of densely packed pine trees reared up on both sides and, rather than make the scenery look ominous, the dark clouds and rain only seemed to magnify its natural beauty and mystery. Not known to me then but I would again follow this path, take in the same beauty around me thirteen months later with a very different result.

The rest of the journey went smoothly without problem and, without running out of fuel we returned to the same border crossing that we had encountered at the start of our journey. The same officers that looked more like Hollywood extras checked our papers and solemnly waved us through into Croatia and within thirty minutes we were parking the car at the hotel where we had collected it and made our way to the apartment.

The next two days were spent simply enjoying the sun and wandering around the seafront and market more to pass time than for enjoyment or relaxation. In truth I yearned to return home as quickly as possible. My heart was heavy in disappointment and by being so close to my goal only seemed to exaggerate my feeling.

Thankfully the two days passed and we landed at Manchester without delay or problem.

On the journey back home I began to realise that maybe I was to find nothing like everyone had told me throughout my search. That I was merely wasting my time, that the man simply had no past, or that his past had been erased forever.

Down hearted I began to accept this over the coming days and pondered that maybe they were correct. That I had sat searching for something that simply was not there nor had ever been. I felt like the monster or UFO hunter that never actually gets to experience a sighting of their own but relies more on other peoples accounts to fulfil their dreams and hopes.

Though down this road we've been so many times

Over following weeks I gathered my now far flung thoughts together and mapped out exactly what I had achieved in all the time that I had searched. In stark truth I had nothing more than what had always been here when he was alive. I had documents relating to his resettlement from Displaced Persons camps in Italy, Germany and the UK which outlined basic information. I had photographs taken before the war and one item of correspondence from a sister in law who, in the immediate years following World War 2 had been living in Montenegro.

The realisation dawned that I had in fact achieved nothing other than what I had gleaned from this country.

The blog pages that I had created in the hope of having just that one hit that recognised anything in relation to my search had not come forth despite over twenty thousands visitors, most of which had been given links from Yugoslavian Genealogy forums.

Private Genealogy Investigators based in the former Yugoslavia had found no connection despite numerous telephone calls to families with the same surname in Croatia, Bosnia and Serbia. Chetnick historians in Serbia had been contacted but they too could find no trace of Ćulumović in the 2nd Korpus Ravna Gore that grandfather had been photographed with near to the town of Čacak in Serbia.

Despite the complete lack of progress I would find myself drawn to the search as if being pushed along and directed by unseen hands. It would feel like a warm magnetic pull willing me to dig that little bit deeper to uncover what was really there and had been there all along throughout my search, but was shrouded from me.

I would refer to the photographs that I had in my possession. There were photographs from the early 1950's where it appeared Maksim would pose without problem and then the photographs of an ailing man several years before his death in the 1980's.

I recall in my adolescent years that it was forbidden to take any photographs of granddad and that he would shy away instantly if any camera came into view.

It became apparent whilst I researched that almost no photographs exist of the man in between his initial arrival to the UK to his last years in the 1980's. Also I recall that he would often change his appearance, he would shave his head and grow a moustache or at times a full beard. I would ask him why the shaven head or beard and he would simply imply that this was for religious purposes. Knowing otherwise this was always accepted as a satisfactory answer and the mild curiosity would be settled.

The answer I may have uncovered during my research is simply that he was afraid. Post war Yugoslavia under Josip Broz had built a highly efficient Secret Police known as the UDBA. Anyone considered by the organisation to be enemies of the country would be targeted and assassinated. Individuals that had fled Yugoslavia could be, depending on their reasons for exile considered enemies of the socialist regime and there are records of international assassinations including killings in the UK.

Maybe this was the true reason for the secrecy that enveloped him wherever he went.

Although he would never speak about anything during the war it was obvious that he was a highly respected figure in the Serbian community.

My parents recall that whenever he entered a room everyone would rise without hesitation and that in group conversation everyone would speak English if he was in the room, as soon as he left the conversation would switch to their native Serbian tongue and English would only be spoken again when he entered the room again. Mother always had the impression that the reason for this strange ritual was that whilst he was not present he did not want anything to be understood in case something was spoken that could give any hint of the secrets he carried with him.

The following months were spent feeling downhearted and beaten. I started the search with little, if any hope of ever finding out any information as this had been so closely guarded throughout granddads life. As I progressed my hopes had been constantly raised and then sent crashing down again as if on a never ending rollercoaster. I had however always bounced back with determination and resilience and simply picked up the pieces of the puzzle and started again. This time I felt truly beaten and the air of defeat must have been apparent in an email I sent to the online friend in Zagreb who had helped me so much, out of sheer kindness wherever he could. He replied that despite every set back, every dead end that I had encountered he had never felt such a feeling of defeat in the letter that I had sent him. He urged me to continue and that this was just another stumbling block that should not halt me in what I was attempting to do.

His reply filled me with renewed vigour and fuelled my desire even more to complete the journey that I had embarked and to take my search to the end of its course regardless. He urged me to pick up the pieces from the very beginning and re-asses the threads of information that I had collected in my possession. The one piece of evidence that I had did have was the photograph that had been sent from Bijelo Polje in Montenegro. Strangely this had been signed by a sister in-law, a sister in-law that looked almost identical to another photograph that had been signed as being from his wife.

The friend in Zagreb kindly contacted the local radio station in Bijelo Polje to see if they could either shed some light on the story or to see if the people in the photograph could be identified by residents living there. Despite the photographs and correspondence being circulated know one came forth either to offer any information or to acknowledge any recognition of the people photographed. Yet another lead in my search had come to a close. The vital and only lead that connected real people to a real place.

Throughout these months I would constantly check, double check, and check again the paperwork and photographs that I had. It was always the photographs that would draw my gaze. It was always the photographs that would keep the reality of my search fuelled. I would look into the eyes in an attempt to decipher any secrets that may be hidden there, but found none only the memories of a man that had no past to read.

The photographs would draw me back, back to the times of his life. Each time I would curse and regret deeply that I had not pushed him a little when he had announced that he was to write a book. The memories would have been in those pages and maybe the mystery would have been solved without the need for looking any further.

I turned full circle once again in my search and again looked at the other villages in both Bosnia and Serbia with the name Brđani. I mailed tourist boards from the areas that covered the villages but got no reply.

Hours each day I would spend scanning the internet for any clues that might lead me to what I searched.

Then came the breakthrough, the ultimate breakthrough that within months would not only lead me to what I desperately searched but would also see me walking the footsteps I longed for in Bosnia.

I had corresponded online with a photographer that had posted his work focusing on the Pliva region. He had lived in the town of Šipovo prior to the civil war and recalled that although he had no recollection of any Ćulumović families from that area he did know of a Ćulum that had lived in the village of Brđani. Ostoja Ćulum had been a well known and respected figure he went onto say and had died twenty years previously. He said that children would shout "chulum" whenever he walked passed and that he would hold a captive audience with his amusing stories wherever he went.

The name Chulum jolted me and my mind raced back to the first meeting with the surviving chetnick. I remember passing him a photograph of granddad and how he had reacted with the word "Chulum". I remember even more how the man's wife and almost spat the words "That was not his name" and how

the man had instantly withdrawn. I was later to find that granddad had been a very good friend of the man's wife and that they had known each other before the outbreak of war.

I passed this information to the friend in Zagreb and to the investigators that I had been using in Montenegro.

The friend in Zagreb, efficient as usual replied back the next day with renewed hope and enthusiasm. It was again obvious that he had given up some of his own precious free time to help me in my now desperate search. He passed onto me e-mail addresses that he had found online of Ćulum families living in and around the Mirkonjic Grad area, a town north of Šipovo. As he suggested I emailed each of the names listed, about twenty in total, explaining briefly my search for family information and asking if they had any connection or knowledge of Ćulum families having lived in the village of Brđani.

Agonizing weeks crept slowly by as I checked and rechecked my inbox constantly. My hopes were fading and yet again I felt the air of defeat engulfing me as yet another hopeful lead was slipping from my grasp. When all appeared to have lost and this latest lead looking like it was to head the same way as countless others I received an email. It was from a Ćulum family and, although not related to my search did verify that there had been families with the name living in Brđani and that they would visit the village to try and solve the question I had posted.

The weeks again slowly ran there cycle with nothing more. Like the rollercoaster I felt that I had again reached the dizzy heights only to be hurtled earthwards to disappointment after the excitement of the ride. Just as I felt that I was reaching the summit prior to fall the rollercoaster stopped with the mail I received from the family.

They apologized for the lateness it read but they had information that I was so desperate to find.

During a trip into Šipovo they had traveled the four miles into the village and had spoke with an elderly woman. Astonishingly the woman remembered Maksim when asked if she knew anything that could be of any assistance. Remarkably, given the passing of sixty years she relayed to the family that Maksim had indeed lived in the village but had disappeared during World war two. As to his whereabouts she had never known only that she had never seen or heard of him since.

She also verified that Maksim was the younger brother to Ostoja Ćulum and kindly walked with the family to show them not only the grave of Ostoja but also the family house that was remarkably still standing. Even more remarkable the elderly woman could recall long lost events from the family's history. She relayed that only the two brothers and a daughter had survived a brutal and murderous attack on the village in 1941. That Ostoja had remarried but after his death in 1987, the wife had moved to Serbia. More importantly that there were indeed living relatives whom she would somehow make contact to pass on that someone was desperate to make long lost contact.

I read, and re-read the short paragraph over and over. I simply could not take in the short paragraph that was before me. So many years of relentless searching and constant disappointments and here was a living person that could actually remember granddad on his native soil.

Four photographs were attached to the email. With shaking hands I selected the first and waited with baited breath. I was drawn and transfixed to the image that opened in front of me. It was a house perched on a gentle slope of grass and plum trees. The structure was fashioned from wood with a stone base and steeply pointed roof. It was the kind of house that conjured up images of the children's novel Hansel and Gretel. Here was the man. In one photograph I knew for sure that I had finally found what I had so desperately searched. His very essence and fabric poured from the wooden structure.

I was drawn back to the wooden sheds that he had built on his beloved allotment. This little house was there in each and every one of them and I now realized that he had replicated everything that he knew and loved. That he had cocooned himself in the surroundings that he had felt safe and secure and that he had built himself a piece of his past here so far from his true home.

The photograph conjured images of the man that he had been. A simple man living out a simple existence of which he had loved and lost. A man whose own destiny had been changed forever in one night of hatred and murder and could never be returned.

The second photograph was that of a grave. Ostoja Ćulum stared with eyes fixed from the cabriole china photograph embosomed on the marker. Here was the brother that granddad had spoken so fondly of in his early memories from childhood. How they had got drunk on stolen plum brandy and smoked in secret the cigarettes made from corn husks. Like that of the house I knew that for the first time I was looking deep into the very memories that had followed the man to his death. That I was seeing what he has seen and felt before he was torn from the people and surroundings that he knew. How sadness filled me with the knowing that the two brothers would spend the rest of their natural lives never knowing of the others continued life and that their thoughts would have continued daily for over forty years until their passing within twelve months of each other.

The third and fourth photographs were of the elderly lady stood by the house.

The information simply would not sink in and I scrutinized every word looking for anything that could be incorrect as if wanting to find a mistake that meant that my search was not over. It was as if I wanted the search to be incomplete and simply could not face the fact that I was nearing what I always thought as being the impossible. I would now sit for days looking at the writing, scanning the photographs for clues that were not there.

Realization slowly sank in and I faced the fact that there were many factors which pointed to the information being correct.

How it had been staring at me for so long without me ever knowing. The name Chulum that he had been known and even in his early signatures, the clues were there. He would write Ćulum as if in bold and a much lighter ović as if he had momentarily forgotten his name and had added this as an afterthought.

The weeks slowly passed with nothing further. I was now so close but needed final closure to put to rest what I had started so long ago. This could now only come with actual contact with living relatives of Maksim's in Bosnia.

This had never been my goal but now things had progressed so much and had entered a very different phase. Throughout my entire life I had been told over and over again that everyone had been killed during World War two and that there was nothing left there. My only desire had been to trace the birth place and visit so that I could see for myself what he had gazed at when he woke each day.

Now things were very different with the realization that he had in fact family that had survived. Not only had they survived that night of utter carnage when the village had been destroyed but would have lived out the horrors when history had repeated itself during the years of civil war in the 1990's.

Maksim's life had not only continued in his beloved homeland but had also flourished whilst he had spent his days in solitude for what could have been. Again I would look for clues from the memory that I retain as to whether the man knew deep down in his own mind that close ties remained there, or had he simply accepted that death had marched its merry dance across those he had once known, cherished and loved dearly.

Just has I was starting to get over the initial shock that I was nearing the end to my search I received an email. I could not believe what I was reading and would have to read it over and over again to comprehend the short message.

It was from Mile, Ostoja Ćulum's grandson. He verified that Maksim had been the lost brother and knew from family stories that he had escaped to England. Mile went onto to say that he had read, with interest my blog pages with information and details of my search.

He expanded that he would like very much to speak with me and gave me a contact telephone number that I should call. Although he spoke very little English his youngest son, Sasha did, and that I should telephone when he was home, anytime after 6pm.

My natural impatience ness got the better of me and I could wait no longer. I dialled the telephone number with trembling hands at 5.30pm. I was so nervous when I heard the pulsing of the connecting telephone on the other end of the line and so very nearly replaced the receiver in its cradle when I was stopped by the sound of a woman's voice in Bosnian. Cautiously I said hello and that I was wanting to speak with Mile. Words I could not understand were spoken back in return and again I said the name Mile and that I was calling from England. I could hear fumbling and voices and then I heard someone say "Hello, how are you?" in broken English. The male voice relayed that his name was Saša and that he was Mile's son. He went onto say that Mile was there with him in the room but that he would translate the conversation. It was obvious that the family were delighted that Maksim had indeed survived as they had been told and that now, after all the years that had passed they would learn of his life following his final departure from Bosnia.. In that very first conversation, I was made so welcome and invited to travel to Bosnia where I would be a welcome guest and that finally I would get to visit the very place that I had desired for so long. I had would see, feel and experience what granddad had done so in the innocence of his youth.

We arranged that I would telephone again the following week and I would check available flights to Sarajevo without further delay.

I then received another email. The subject read – "Petra's daughter." For some reason this email stared out at me from the rest and I was immediately drawn to it. I remember the strange feelings of apprehension as I clicked on the message to read its content. I waited with baited breath and then read the short message. It was from Vesna, Mile's sister. Her mother had been Petra, the daughter to Ostoja Ćulum. Vesna had spoken to Mile about me and had visited the blog pages that I had online. She explained that she had suffered the same fate as Maksim had and had fled Bosnia to live in the USA. It saddened me to think yet again the same family, albeit different generations had been displaced through warfare and the saying that history repeats itself certainly rang true here.

I waited until morning before I dialed the telephone number that had been included in the email. I was unsure of the time difference between the UK and USA but for some reason had assumed that the time zone in the States was in front of our own.

The first call was at 9am but there was no reply and I left a brief message on the answer phone. When I arrived at work I was dismayed to find that I had been wrong and that the USA was well behind out time and that I had called in the early hours of the morning. Later that day I received a voice message on my mobile phone. It was Vesna asking me to telephone her.

With trembling hands I carefully dialed the number and waited, with baited breath I listened to the pulsating ring tone. After what seemed like an eternity I heard a woman's voice say hello. I introduced myself and the excitement was evident in both our voices as we exchanged pleasantries.

Vesna explained that she had been told of Maksim by her mother and that she had known that he had indeed survived the war and had lived on in England. Her mother had spoke of him and had said that she could remember that letters from England had been sent early after the war, but that these letters had been destroyed by the authorities before they could be read.

She had always known, as her father, Ostoja had, that Maksim had indeed survived the war and had been displaced somewhere in England.

I knew instantly in that moment that I had found the connection to what I had so desperately searched.

Even the name Petra raised the hairs on my neck. The name, for whatever reason had been instilled in my childhood memory. If I ever envisaged a

Yugoslavian woman in my minds eye then she was always called Petra. Why I do not know as granddad had never once used this name in his faltered recollections to all of his early life.

Petra had been the mother of Maksim. The mother that he had fondly recalled as being in constant hiding from him as he searched out her breast milk up until the age of seven years old. Petra had been the name that Maksim's brother, Ostoja, had passed down to his own daughter. The daughter Petra, whose own children in Bosnia remain now to complete and carry on my own story into print with the much awaited factual evidence I so desired.

As the following days slowly unfolded my initial excitement turned to a deep inner feeling of dread. I had never once in my search imagined that I would actually meet and speak with real live people that were connected to Maksim. I had searched only the soil, not the flesh. It was now the living that I had broken through to and not the pasts of yesterday and remembering.

Vesna seemed as compelled as I was that I should travel to Bosnia and finally come face to face with Brđani. She spoke to her brother for me and bridged the language barrier. Mile readily invited me to visit him in his home town of Novi Travnik and offered that he would collect me at the airport in Sarajevo, have me as his guest in his apartment and would drive me to the birthplace of granddad.

Over the following weeks, with the help, support and enthusiasm of Vesna my trip was arranged. I had flight tickets to Sarajevo and she arranged the details that I would see my often fruitless search draw to successful close.

I will always been indebted to her for this and feel that she was the final piece that was to fit and secure the puzzle into place once and for all.

Chapter Five – The long Road to Brđani

WITH EVERYTHING IN PLACE I set off once again from the dark streets of Featherstone. This time I was alone, so very alone to face whatever destiny had to offer. This time I would travel without the company and security of others. I had shaken mother's foreboding from my shoulders and dismissed her repeated appeals and financial rewards for me to turn my back on the search and to remain here, safe in the place I knew and understood.

I had traveled so far now and could not simply turn my back on what I had desired for so long.

This time the farewells were absent as I loaded the overnight bag into the car and drove slowly away. The traffic was relatively light on the M62 motorway which winds itself across the isolated Peninnes, the high ridge that separates the counties of Yorkshire and Lancashire and is regarded as the very backbone of England.

Slowly I drifted down with the road into the urban sprawl of Manchester and joined the traffic towards the airport. Satellite Navigation is my own savior and surprisingly the car found its own way to its allocated parking place at terminal one.

The taxi was prompt and with a final cigarette I entered the building of no return. Maybe I fumbled my way through everything there I cannot recall in my excitement. I recall stopping at duty free; I bought perfume for Mira and scotch for Mile. Looking back, maybe scotch whiskey was a poor choice to give to a man that distills is very own superior brandy but my heart was in the choice.

The smoking ban weighed heavily on me there as I waited for my flight to flash its presence on the departure boards. Oh god I could have loved then the comfort of a smoke but no. New laws maybe have gone crazy so no nicotine whilst I waited so anxiously for the short journey that had now taken me twenty years to travel.

With the rush of modern air travel I had little time to ponder and was ushered, onto a waiting transporter of the skies.

Despite my inner reservations and fears of traveling alone all was quite well. I was seated with a teenage German girl that spoke probably more fluent English than I actually did. She was based at school in England and spent the whole flight talking of her schooling and showing me the photographs of the castle looking place of education that her parents were obviously heavily investing for her future success.

Maybe one day she will read this and think yes or maybe one day I will read of her. Either way I hope it is either of us that will finally be successful in our lives.

The short flight passed without problems and we touched down smoothly at Munich airport.

I had seven hours now until my connecting flight to Sarajevo and wandered through the shops looking for nothing in particular only for the passing of time.

I spent time chatting to a Brazilian guy who was waiting for his own connecting flight home after visiting Italy. We smoked and drank crisp German beer as we rattled away in broken English and the hours slowly drifted by until it was time for a final farewell as I headed for my own departure.

The aircraft was only half booked so I chose to sit alone at the rear. At least here I thought if something catastrophic was to happen I would be the last to perish. The same disillusioned thought had followed me in my career as a coal miner. Whenever I was to descend the vertical shaft I would choose to stand on the upper deck of the man riding lift, if disaster struck on its descent, I would be the last to perish.

The hour long flight soon passed and the aircraft dipped its nose in descent. I scanned the dark ground beneath and could make out the clusters of twinkling lights from the houses on the hillsides and began to feel nervous for the first time.

The realization was sinking into me that within minutes I would meet the family that Maksim had lost so long ago. I remembered how lonely he had looked when he was working the land on the allotment. How he had tried so hard to fit into the English way of life but never seemed to get there. It saddened me so much to think that when he had been alone to dwell on his thoughts he would have been thinking of the people that he had lost and with stark realization that he would have had to accept that he would never see them again. Now I was to see and meet his lost ones twenty years after he had taken his last dying breath.

My nerves were beating me in the competition to remain calm as I hurried through customs and passport control. I rounded the corner into the arrivals lounge and without having to scan the faces of the people there was instantly drawn to the three figures standing to the left. Mile, Mira and Mile's youngest son, Saša smiled back at my own.

In awkward embrace we greeted each other in turn. My first impressions was that Mile, an imposing figure was full of tenderness and gentleness despite his visible strength. Mira had the eyes that radiated the feeling of love and warmth as we embraced. She looked so deep into my own that, for a brief instant it felt that she was reading my soul. Saša was vibrant and full of energy as most teenagers are. He was the English speaker and most of our mirrored greetings were channeled through him.

I was led outside to the waiting car. I was living now a truly magical moment. I was amongst the people that Maksim had lost. The very people that I had searched for so long and, not only was I now in their very presence, they would lead me also to the soil I so desperately needed to walk.

In the car the conversation was fragmented. Little we knew of the others language and Saša at times found it difficult to translate the eager, hurried words.

We headed north from Sarajevo, rising sharply over serious mountain ridges. These once were the snowy ridges of idyllic winter scenes for tourists, wanting the thrill of the slope. Instead they were deserted, the ghostly figures of the cable car towers a monument to what could have been. Now they stood testament to the horrors that had spread across the once beauty of this magnificent land.

Slowly the road dipped down into descent and the pinpricks of lights flickered before us as we approached the town of Novi Travnik. Gradually the flickering lights grew in size and numbers and houses began to appear along the road.

My first impression of the town was that of its uniformity. The buildings were set out as if by careful planning. Everything was in blocks of squares as it they had been set out on grid lines. The whole town was if it had been set out on a surveyor's desk and that nothing more had been added to the plan since its design.

It was only after my visit that I read that as its layout suggested, the town had been purposely built to serve the ammunition and armaments factory nearby.

Within minutes of entering the town we came to a stop outside a four storey tenement block. This was Mile's home and he gestured for me to get out of the car. Like a gentleman he collected my suitcase and beckoned me to the entrance.

I was drawn to the neatly stacked piles of chopped firewood that festooned the whole buildings facade. As I looked at the neighboring tenements this echoed

And each one had its own ready supply. My mind instantly regressed again to granddads life. He too was obsessed with the need to chop and store wood for burning through the cold winter months. In his final years this became an obsession and the basement of his house was so full of kindling that it took weeks for us to clear away, following his death. To the ordinary eye this may not appear strange, just an old man preparing himself for the winter months. As a retired coalminer however he had not the need to make such ambitious efforts to protect himself from the rigors of winter. It was, at that time, the government's duty to provide all coal miners, either still in employment or retired with free fuel to see them through the winter months. Obviously old habits die hard and he was simply going through the motions of his earlier life. Maybe even, reliving his dream of his continued existence there.

Once inside the apartment I was welcomed by Mile's waiting wife who gestured for me to take a seat on the couch. Once seated I was offered a small glass of Slivovitz. Not usually a hard liquor drinker I reluctantly accepted it and, following Mile's lead gulped it down in one. The liquid felt hot as it made its way to my stomach and gave the entire body a deep feeling of inner warmth. Surprisingly for me I enjoyed its rich taste and eagerly offered the glass for a refill when the bottle appeared again on the table. Some months earlier I had watched a movie that had been set in Bosnia. In one scene the actors were in the lobby of a hotel and the waiter brought to the table a bottle of the clear plum brandy. As they drank one of the actors told of a story that whenever Slivovitz is drank the devil sits, unnoticed in a corner of the room laughing. Whether the devil was sat in that room I did not know or care, all I knew was that there I was surrounded by the most kindest people that I have been lucky to meet and I was being welcomed in a way that I will never forget.

The conversation flowed despite the language barrier and photographs of Maksim and Ostoja were exchanged. Although Maksim had been the larger of the two it was obvious the physical similarities of brotherhood. They spoke at length of their grandfather, how he had strived hard all of his life, his humour and most of all his stubbornness.

Stubbornness was evidently a family trait. Granddad was the most stubborn person I have ever come across. If he declared that he was right from the beginning then right he would have to be to the end and I had learned from an early age that co amount of discussion would change his opinion so it was always easier just to go along with what he had suggested. I recall one manifestation of this stubbornness in particular. He had blamed a workman who was erecting a wall at the top of the street for the dampness that had occurred in his cellar. No amount of logic could persuade him from what he thought so he set out, hammer in hand to confront the poor man. I remember how I had laughed at the spectacle of the poor workman laying down a newly mortared brick only to have it smashed with a heavy blow from the hammer. Not wanting to be outdone the workman replaced the brick only to have this again smashed into fragments. The scene went on and on and when the Police finally arrived the pair were standing amidst a pile of rubble and dust. Granddad was duly arrested and was taken to the local Police station. Had it not been for mothers never ending pleas to the authorities he would have been charged with criminal damage and placed before the local magistrate for sentence.

I would later learn from Vesna, Ostoja's granddaughter that he too had a reckless side to his character like his brother and that his antics continue to amuse the fireside drinking of the younger generations to this day.

Ostoja, in his prime years was a keen horseman and had trained one particular horse to run from its grazing when whistled and kneel in front of the door to the house to be mounted. Ostoja had heard that a nearby family was holding a party. Intrigued as to where his own invite was he stepped outside and whistled his trusty mare. True to form the animal heard its masters call and galloped to the house and kneeled before him. Ostoja rode the few miles to where the celebration was taking place and an altercation, for whatever reason occurred and he was not allowed entry. Solemnly he returned home and, through the night thought of ways that would teach the family a lesson they would never forget and, any future nights of mirth and merriment they held he would be accepted with open arms.

Early the following morning he returned to the house and, making sure that the occupants had left on their daily chores set about planting explosives around the doorway. Watching from a safe distance the explosives were ignited and he returned home, happy in the knowing that any future parties that the family held he would always now be at the top of their invitation list for fear of reprisal!

As the stories and Slivovitz flowed, Mile's wife, Dushka quietly busied herself, adorning the table with food. For so few people I have never seen so much food. Boiled potatoes, freshly baked bread, salamis, cold meats and the tradition Bosnian dish of Sarma. Sarma is a dish of meat and rice, mixed together and wrapped in cabbage leaves. Although I had never seen this prepared dish before, I was told by mother, after my visit that this had been regularly cooked by granddad when she was a child.

The good food, hot liquor, conversation and excellent company only seemed to speed up the passing of time and all too soon it was time to retire. I was told that the day would begin at 6am with the hour long journey by car to the village of Brđani. Tired from the long day of travel and a little intoxicated I soon drifted into a deep sleep only to be roused what felt like minutes later to be informed that it was time to wake and have coffee before we were to leave on the final leg of my journey that was to take me to the final place of my search.

Over coffee I was told that there had been a slight change of plan for the day. Mile would not be driving but he had invited a friend of his who was to take the wheel for the drive north.

Off into the Darkness of Uncertainty

The sweet aroma and taste of Turkish coffee was all too soon interrupted with the sound of a car tooting its horn outside. I was told that our transport had arrived and that we should hurry as the journey could be long in the worsening weather.

Outside Mile gestured me in to the waiting van that had parked outside. He followed and I sat between the driver and him. Words were exchanged that I had no understanding and the driver smiled in acknowledgement as I picked out the word "Andy" in the quick fire conversation.

We drove steadily through the uniform lay out of the town which appeared relatively deserted and has the houses and tenements grew less in numbers I saw for the first time the huge and imposing structure of the Bratstvo Armaments factory. To say huge would be a gross understatement, it was colossal. Despite having been born and raised in the heavy industries of Yorkshire I had never seen anything on this scale. This truly must have been the very jewel in the crown of the rising socialist Yugoslavia in its time of birth and construction. Driving steadily past, in the darkness and fog it now appeared such a sad monument to what had tragically followed its spectacular rise. It had become now a shattered dream, its mammoth entirety was lifeless and in the steady rot of decline. This decline however, unlike the industries in my own country had not been triggered by bad managements of government or world recession. This rot was the result of mans ability to hate his fellow man. Here stood Bosnia as it was. Years of barbarity, killing and destruction was the result of this jewels demise. It and its people had been bombed out of existence but, unlike its people the structure could not be simply hidden from sight and would remain a constant witness for all to see. Maybe, I thought in sadness, Bratstvo should remain and be preserved to remind mankind what we are truly capable of and that lessons should be learned from there to carry on to the next generations that may be forced to endure the same fears and loss as had the people here.

Driving onwards we left the sadness of Bratstvo behind and the road steadily climbed into the darkness. As we rose the fog was met with the high lying mist and this only added to the uncertainty and gloom that was now setting deeply into my thoughts.

Listening to the unrecognizable conversation within the vehicle my mind began to take on the wanderings of possibilities. With a deep lurch of the heart I suddenly had the terrible thought that maybe; just maybe my own stubbornness may have taken me now too far. I was no longer in control of anything and had witnessed, with the factory that Bosnia was capable of anything. I had been warned countless times to let things be and not to dig into the past. That I should celebrate the life that I had known, with the man that I revered so much and, not to delve into the past that he had fought to keep hidden for so long.

Each thought now seemed to accelerate into the next and for one awful moment I accepted that here I was to finally meet the fate that Maksim had escaped for so long. That I was to be punished for the possible old scores that were left undone. The continued secrecy of his life, the death threats on the forums, the attempts to force my rental car from the road during my previous visit all came together in that instant. Even mother had offered me the price of the airfares to persuade me from traveling again.

Everything around me now only exaggerated my rigid thoughts? Why a van and not a car. Why the sudden change of plan with the driver?

My wild and irrational thoughts crashed back to reality with the words "Andy, Bon Bon?" I looked at Mile's smiling face and he gestured with outstretched hand offering me a boiled sweet. I accepted with thanks and sucked on the slightly warming taste of fruits with relish.

Mile offered me the same confectionary at Sarajevo airport on my departure and poured them into my open palm until I could hold no more. These kept me company throughout my return journey and will now be a constant reminder of the kindness that he had shown to me during my initial stay with him and his family.

The road gradually descended into a steeply sided river valley which seemed vaguely familiar to me from my previous visit there. We headed north and soon the darkness and fog gave way to daylight. We passed two houses that remained burnt out, relics from the war. These I definitely recognized as on my previous visit I had used them as a backdrop to a photograph I had taken.

In the gloom we rounded a sharp corner and Mile drew my attention and pointed out to the right. Even in the gloom of early morning the waterfalls at Jajce were a spectacular sight. At Jajce the river Pliva meets the river Vrbas and cumulates into a beautiful crescendo of water. It was 30 meters high, but during the war, the area was flooded and the waterfall is now 20 meters high. The flooding may have been due to an earthquake and/or attacks on the hydroelectric power plant further up the river.

Heading south from Jajce I noticed for the first time that the road signs were now written in the Cyrillic alphabet. This was a clear indication that we had crossed the invisible line from the Bosnian Croat Federation and had entered into the Serbian Republic.

Before long we had entered the town of Šipovo. The same town that twelve months prior I had reached but had got no further in my findings. The van came to a stop outside a bar and we entered to be greeted by the owner. The four people who were sat in the corner looked up as we passed and nodded before returning to their own quick fire conversation. The owner invited us to sit at a table and beckoned the waitress who hurriedly brought Slivovitz and Turkish coffee. Although not usually a drinker of hard liquor at 8am I followed suit and drank down the fiery liquid in one. The bar owner immediately beckoned again the waitress who brought more glasses to the table. This would be the ritual for the next hour.

Although little of the conversation could be understood I would pick out the repeated reference to the name "Ćulum" and that glasses would be raised in obvious toast to the name, repeatedly.

Slowly but surely the effects of the brandy ebbed its way into my brain and acted like a translator. It was if I could now understand what was being said in conversation and would nod in agreement when I was being spoken to. All too soon it was time to move onto our next destination and, bidding our farewells to others in the bar we departed. Leaving Šipovo behind the van turned onto a white, chalk track that snaked its way into the surrounding hillside.

We pulled over at the side of a small stretch of iron railings. There were maybe twenty grave markers dotted about in the rough grass. One of them was that of Ostoja, granddads lost brother. The same marker that the kind family had sent me photographs of some months before. A candle was lit and we stood in respect offering a moments silence before continuing our journey along the crudely made track.

Slowly rounding a corner I saw for the first time the house. I recognized it instantly from the photographs but was surprised that it stood alone. I had known that the village had been raised to the ground during the attack in 1941 but had expected other dwellings to have been erected in their place. The house looked so alone, perched on the hillside and surrounded by the long grass.

We left the van and walked down the grassy slope towards the building that I had only dreamed of seeing through my very own eyes. This was the very house that Maksim's brother had lived until his death twenty years previous. Its rustic charm pulsed its way into my soul and, closing my eyes for one second I took in its very fabric and felt its atmosphere in the air around me.

Mile opened the door and gestured for me to enter. It was much smaller inside than I had imagined. Walking through a narrow passageway I was surprised just how well constructed it was despite the quaint crudeness of its exterior. There was one single living room which was adjoined by the sleeping quarters.

An idle wood burning stove sat in a corner and I imagined the heat and mouth watering aromas that would have been given out in happier times with family meals being cooked over laughter and conversation.

Although the house had probably not been directly connected to Maksim I could almost feel him there. He would have known of the house and that it would have been a similar structure that he had lived nearby with his own wife and family before the cruel night that had changed his life then forever. I dwelled on the rolling views across the countryside that he too would have seen through his very own eyes and I marveled on the beauty that was set out before me.

How I wished in that one moment that I would have been faster in my search. Four simple letters had kept me from this for so long. The added "ovic" at the end of the name had thwarted and mislead me over the years of my quest to uncover the truth behind the man. The passing of time not only fogs out old memories but also sees the passing of the very people that I had searched. As each year had passed so too had the knowledge of those left behind and it would have only been a matter of time until nothing, not even that beautiful rustic house on the lush hillside of Brđani would have survived to tell the story.

The house was set on a steep slope and from the front had only one storey. Sloping down to the rear it opened into a two storey structure. The base made from rough stone and the upper of years old, seasoned, dark timber.

The lower stone section, now dormant would have had multiple uses in its former days. Here would be stored the tools and everyday equipment that would have been used around the farm. Livestock would be herded in during the harsh winter months, not only to protect them from the rigours of nature but would also serve as a primitive form of central heating, giving the occupants above the much needed warmth from the animal's body temperature, happy and snug below.

The land around the house was overgrown, nature slowly taking back what was rightfully hers. I imagined a very different scene that would have been set out in happier times past. Chickens scratching the earth for their own livelihood, eking out the scraps of food that were on offer. Lambs bleating out their own chorus and the smell of wood being burned as slowly damson plums were being distilled in the home brewed distillation of the fiery brandy that everyone continues to produce in the area.

Despite the onslaught of winter the sheer freshness and uplifting vigour that the place held was still present and I so wanted to stay there, captive in its ambience. Mile interrupted my thoughts and motioned towards the waiting van that sadly it was time to leave.

We continued our journey along the chalk white track for maybe five miles and drew to a steady stop alongside a single storey, modern brick house that stood in a cluster of a handful of similar dwellings.

At the entrance to the house I was met with the smiling and welcoming faces of a man and an elderly woman. Without word I was welcomed inside and offered a seat and no sooner as I was seated the customary shot of plum brandy was offered, and by now, readily accepted. Through struggling, broken English Mile introduced the woman as Borka, the daughter of granddads sister, Sava. Although I had never recalled granddad ever mentioning any sister, on my return home to England, mother verified this and said that, yes, there had been in fact two sisters. The man was then introduced as Maksim, her son and that Borka had in fact given him the same name as her uncle, the ever missed brother that her own mother would speak about throughout her natural life.

Through the haze of constant shots of Slivovitz I will remember Borka as if she were sat now at my side as I write. The eyes and smile were that of Maksim himself and I would constantly be drawn into her gaze as if by magnetism. There was a sparkle to her eyes that I had nor seen for over twenty years and would seem to draw the inner child out of me each time that we connected in glance.

All too soon it was time to leave the comfort of that little house and with a final farewell and tear in my eye I was shown into the car of Maksim, Borka's son. As before I had no idea where we were headed and with the brandy racing through my brain, nor did I care. I knew now that I was amongst the most sincere and welcoming people that I had ever met. That these were the people that had retained the true human feelings of kindness, the feelings that sadly, have been lost to so many of us.

The day finished in a haze of alcohol, good food and the best company that any man could wish for. I was taken to the home of Maksim's, to meet his wife and children. My recollections there are few as by now the Slivovitz had taken a heavy toll on my senses. I remember the hospitality shown to me and giving out the collection of Euros that I had accumulated at Munich airport, to the children.

I remember then only being back in Novi Travnik, Mile's apartment. I remember vividly Mira being there and how we had the tears that only happiness gives as we held hands and looked into each others eyes. The bridge had finally been rebuilt in that moment and I had finally brought granddad home to the family that he had lost so long ago.

I remember then the voice of Mile waking me and saying that it was time to get ready for the journey back to Sarajevo airport. Maybe the story of the devil and Slivovitz was true after all, but in my case he had waited till the morning before he sat laughing in the corner. I had the worst hangover possible and my head screamed out each time my thirsty mouth gulped down the offered coffee.

With a sad farewell I waved to the kind family that had offered so much hospitality to me and settled myself in the small car for the journey to Sarajevo where I had landed just thirty six hours before.

The journey passed slowly and I was saddened that my short stay had come to a close. At the airport Mile refused to leave until my flight was announced and I made my way through passport control and customs. In one final gesture of kindness he beckoned me to hold out my open palm. In doing so he handed me some of the Bon Bons that he had offered as we had set out the previous morning on our trip to Brđani. This one simple gesture will stay forever ingrained in my memory as a sign of true kindness that man can show to his fellow man.

Twelve hours later I arrived back to my home in Featherstone. The trip that had taken twenty years to organise had sadly finished in the blink of an eye.

There will, of course be more trips to that beautiful place but as memories go, nothing will ever outdo those that I hold for those short moments that I spent there that weekend.

Probably taken at Camp Bagnola, Naples Italy. The first of three Displacement camps that Maksim was held following the end of World War 2

Enjoying the sun. Maksim pictured lying down at front with a group of other displaced refugees near to the Miner's Hostel in Castleford, England.

Ostoja Ćulum 1905 – 1987, the elder brother that remained in Bosnia following World War 2.

Maksim Ćulumović 1909 – 1988, the younger brother who remained in England until his death. Sadly the two brothers would never again have any contact following World War 2.

Petra Ćulum, daughter of Ostoja pictured with husband Ilija Pljuco.

Photograph taken of Christmas festivities at the Miner's Hostel Castleford England. Granddad is pictured far right with Nana second from right at the front.

The house of Ostoja Ćulum in the village of Brđani. Ostoja lived here until his death in 1987.

Petra Pljuco (Ćulum) pictured with daughters Mira and Vesna (center).

Mile and Vesna during the war years in Bosnia.

Last photograph taken at my wedding at Pontefract. Granddad was terminally ill and within six months of the photograph he had passed away.

Chapter Six – Catching the Coin

Remember when you were young,

WHEN THE COIN IS TOSSED it will always show the winning side as it stops spinning. Stories too can have a hidden side that sometimes can never be seen unless we scratch at the surface and look closely for the hidden clues that are offered.

My own story is like the coin, having two sides that were never to be seen together. I would sit and ponder and, maybe dream of the other side of the story, always in wander what it would be like and, if the other side ever existed at all.

Without the strong unknown pull that drew me to uncover what was there I would never have found the coins second face and, without this deep desire the story would never have been there to unfold and to understand finally.

I would spend lazy summer days on granddads allotment simply staring at the blue sky and imagining being in Yugoslavia. What it was really like there and if the people far away were simply seeing the same clouds at the same time as what I saw. I would never accept, as the others did, that there was nothing there that everyone connected had gone without trace, and the story was lost in the annals of time.

Finally the coin as been tossed, only now it has landed

on neither side but shows both as if they have always been together, side by side, each one the ultimate winner in its own right.

This is the side I had longed for so many years and at long last had finally come into view, revealing that my constant search had not been wasted and there were reasons for my strive to uncover.

The following pages are like that of the coin, always having the two faces but only ever showing the one. It is rare, if at all; that the two faces will ever be viewed at the same time and it is a matter of simple physics that the earthly pull will always draw either one of the faces downwards faster than the other. Both faces are connected and were made to be that way, but one will always

look up to the sky in victory whilst the other, face down will look towards the earth in sheer hope and despair of being forgotten. The hope that maybe next time the tide will turn and both will have the opportunity to see the other as they spin and that neither side will win nor lose.

Both sides are now shown. Childhood differences and experiences combine in reunion to cover the tracks of time. Tracks that had been lost, but are now found and shared bring the story together.

From my own humble beginnings in the grimy mining villages of England, to those memories of childhood and teenage years from Vesna. The stories of hope, academic success and then sheer carnage of Bosnia the pages hope to reflect the two sides that have been spun for so long. Maybe now the coin has finally landed on neither side but stands upright in defiance. Both sides can be read together finally and their own knowing of the others existence can be shared and acknowledged as if the coin had never been tossed at all.

The Other Side of Our Life

Looking back I was so happy in my childhood despite the suffering of my parents who were simply trying to make the best of hard times for their children. I will always look back and thank them dearly for the efforts they made and the sacrifices that they would have had to give for out benefit.

My childhood happiness is enveloped in the love of my sister. She is twelve years older and the sort of person that you would only meet once in your lifetime.

Everyone simply adored my big sister and I remember the feelings of jealousy that I felt which I now regret.

I remember being six years old when mom announced that she was to leave for work in Germany. I recall the utter devastation I felt as she told me that she would have to leave so that she could make better money and that she could then buy me nice things and that with the extra money life would be so much better.

With sadness I recollect the following day when she took me to a friend's house where I was to stay. I recall the tears of utter devastation I felt and the innocent childish tantrum that followed.

I refused totally to stay there and demanded, as best that a six year old could that I should be allowed to stay home alone. Maybe the stubbornness is a trait that runs through the blood, rigid had been my grandfather's middle name.

Mom tried her best but I guess the debate was simply not negotiable. I would stay at home despite father working from 6am till 4pm. My brother would be in school and sister was away in Sarajevo.

The memories from those times remain ingrained in my mind and I can still feel the loneliness and hunger I felt as I sat in the window from 6am to fathers return from work at 4pm. He would return with milk and crackers which I would devour feverishly. This was to be the pattern for the next four months until mom returned.

She would tell me for the rest of her life that the four months that she was away she regretted deeply. All the money that she had earned simply went towards paying the bills accrued but she did bring one thing that was so special to me that will stay in my memory for ever. It was a little soft dog that would walk and bark. No other kid had toy like that and I was so proud of there envy. I would proudly strut around knowing he was special and that everyone was so jealous and desired badly what I had got.

So cruel the passing of time can be. The lone and abandoned fighter, fighting his way for freedom through the streets of Featherstone, plastic rife in hand, to the place of his dreams. Toy guns, toy dog, all make believe life that would eventually forge both together in reality and at last both sides would be united.

My Own Little Town

I was born and raised in Novi Travnik (New Town) in Bosnia. The area had been built up at the start of 1949 under the directions of Marshal Tito who wanted to turn his vision of an independent, multi ethnic Yugoslavia. The town was to house workers for the huge Bratstvo armaments factory that, when working at its full capacity would employ more than 11,000 workers. It is said that the town was such a modern place when it was initially constructed that there was no cemetery for the first ten years and was affectionately known as "the town of youth".

I have brother too. Six years older than me. I remember games we played but he was always master, either his rule or nothing. Whatever game we played he was the King, the ruling party. I guess, like all older brothers he was embarrassed of having a little sister that wanted to spend so much time with him and would tell me to leave him in peace and that I was so annoying when he was around his own friends. He would chase me through the house and I would lock myself in the bathroom laughing at his anger.

My father was a very quiet man and would never say a great deal. Maybe this was attributed to mam being such a lively, loud person and he thought it perhaps easier to say little.

When he did speak however it would be the words of a wise and knowing man and his advice was so often if not entirely, the correct advice that I would adhere.

He always said that everyone should have at least one goal in their lives and that his goal was for his three children to successfully complete their schooling.

Looking back to those happy but hard times I can now see just how much was sacrificed by my parents to give us three children the very best start in life that would soon be torn apart by bloodlust and war.

Mother was such a beautiful woman both in essence and looks. Her smile would reach out and warm even the darkest of feelings and lift the spirits of those around her.

Neighbours would comment that whenever she went into town the men would cease their daily business and simply stop and stare as she passed. The woman would become flustered and annoyed that their men folk were so distracted and could be heard scorning them in annoyance.

Although I was extremely proud of mother I was also sometimes a little embarrassed by her at times. She had the habit of always speaking the truth regardless of other people thought. She was courageous and such a brave person, a characteristic that had been moulded as she was growing up by her father, Maksim's lost brother.

She looked up and adored her father so much. I recall that whenever we visited granddad at his house he would be sat waiting on an old wooden bench outside. I was intrigued on each visit how she would kneel in front of him and kiss his outstretched hand. Maybe this is some ancient custom from that place. I do not know but this was how each greeting happened.

How I loved those days spent at granddads house as a little

girl. We would always visit in the summer months. I will never forget the smell of freshly cooked eggs and bread that greeted you as you woke. Even the mere task of first finding the eggs was exciting to me and I would look with anticipation in the corners and spaces under the house in the basement where the hens were kept.

The countryside where granddad lived is breathtakingly beautiful. From the front of the house the view stretches for miles and is only then interrupted by the rising mountains in the far distance. The beauty however is tinged with sadness and evil. Granddad relayed the same story as that told my Maksim. The village had been attacked at the start of World War Two and that mam's mother and brothers and sisters had been brutally beaten to death and the buildings raised to the ground.

I remember on one occasion when we visited granddad listening to the conversation of the adults. I heard mam speak of granddad having a lost brother. This was something completely new to me because I had never heard any mention of a brother before.

Intrigued I asked mam about this brother and she reinforced what I had overheard. She said that yes, granddad did have a brother that had fled to England after world war two and nobody had heard from him since. They had heard that he had tried to send them letters but that these had been withheld by the authorities. No one knew where the brother was, whether he had family, or if he still lived.

My first thought was that I so wanted to know about him and said out loud that he had been so lucky to leave this place and that if I were in his position then I too would never return. Granddad looked at me and, tapping his cane in front of him simply nodded his head and said "Yeah, yeah, brother".

The little house always felt so cosy and warm to me as a child, grandma always seemed to be busying herself cooking whenever I seemed to visit.

They lived a very hard life in harsh conditions that felt so crude to me, being raised in town. I remember there being no bathroom or shower.

One particular day will stay ingrained in my memory forever and I recall it as if it were a scene from yesterday. I was lying down on a blanket at the front of the house when I heard approaching voices and a group of elderly people came into view as they walked down the gentle slope towards the house. Curious I followed them into the house and listened to their babbling conversation. One of the elderly ladies asked granddad "Hey Ostoja have you visited Šipovo recently?" Granddads reply was simply "No, Why?" She went onto say that the town was full of teenagers and that she could not believe that they were kissing openly on benches in broad daylight. So ungodly she went onto say. "So what is wrong with that?" Came his quick reply "See these woods around my house, there is not a single tree that I haven't had you up against!" With that he simply left the room. Everyone broke into laughter including me. The elderly woman jumped so fast as if she had been scolded with hot water, her face glowing the brightest of crimson.

That day, like so many others I remember being so sad when it was time to leave and go back home to town. The way of life there was so different, so slow and lost in time. Just as I was becoming acclimatised to the environment around me and the ways of its people it would come to a close with the inevitable journey home. The following days would be filled with an empty air of loss and wanting. I would miss deeply the cosy little house nestled on the hillside, the woods that were mysterious and inviting for play, the beautiful ice cold water from the wells so pure and above all the sheer silence that enveloped around everything and everyone.

It was so good to spend time there with granddad and grandma. In the gentle images of memory that I have of their farewells I will always see granddad standing at the front of the house, tapping his cane between his feet, grandma would hug me tight, tears in her eyes as she whispered "My cherry pie, I will miss you". Mam would cry too as we left and I would always wander if we would ever see them again.

As a teenager it was always important for me to visit granddad. By doing so I was staying in touch of reality. In town the whole hippy revival was in full swing and I was being drawn into this as most teenagers follow the influences of those around them.

My sister, the ever loving but suspicious mentor kept a close reign on me, so worried that I would fall into the drug culture that raised its head with the music and fashions all around.

Looking back fondly those carefree days were probably the best moments of my life. We lived under the ever watchful eye of socialism, crime was almost non existent and everyone seemed to live together in peace and harmony.

As adults we often think back to the happy times from our younger days and I recall that, although happy and full of energy I always dreamed that one day I would spread my wings and leave the place that I knew so well. I would look up to the sky and my mind would wander and try to visualise the family that were possibly there in England. I knew that granddad had a brother, Maksim and that he had fled there after world war two. With this knowledge I would feel incomplete, as if my very essence had been removed and dissected, being replaced again after the removal of something so important.

Like all teenagers I would at times find myself in conflict with my parents and I would lie awake at night thinking that if only I knew where the lost people were, how I wanted then to find them, to tell them that I was here and longing to move far from this place. With dread I knew that this was not possible and was saddened to think that the same thoughts were maybe being relayed with people in England.

Little did I know back then that at the same time there was someone starting to scratch at the surface and that the scratching would continue for another twenty years and would eventually lift the guarded veil that had been hidden for so long. That the coin would settle at last on the ground but this time both of its sides would be in view of the other.

Although the dreams of being lifted maybe from this place never came I continued to live the happy, hippy life of a kid at school.

I had visions of becoming an interpreter and pursued my knowledge of the English language and hoped that this would give me a good start in life as the English language is widely used all over the world.

Unfortunately my parents did not agree and my high hopes of enrolling at college were stopped in their tracks when they announced that they could not afford the tuition fees at college.

The only alternative for me was to try and get a scholarship but the only academy available was the military academy in Zagreb. My sister whom I looked up for inspiration encouraged me to follow this direction but I was faced with a problem that I would first have to face before I could qualify for a scholarship. Because I had all my hopes pinned on becoming an English interpreter I had not focused amt attention on the subject of mathematics. This was needed in the academy so I was to spend the next two years studying in order that I would qualify. I would seldom leave the house to socialise like the other teenagers in town. Instead I would tirelessly read endless mathematics books and prepare my self for the final examination that would give me the ticket to enter the academy in Zagreb.

Those two years seemed like a living hell to me. I would see and hear the other kids having fun whilst I busied myself in text books. Friends that I had known for years started to avoid me as they saw me as being boring and quite different to them.

I would constantly worry myself with thoughts that all of this may be for nothing and that; maybe I would not even pass the examination.

I look back now and regret that during those two years I

missed out on spending more time visiting my granddad at the house I adored so much. That place has a special place in my heart. It is like a lost world that is cut off from the rigours of everyday life. Nature in that place is everywhere and seems to fill everything with its freshness. It reaches into the soul and draws you in to its tranquillity. I would lie in the grass near to the house and night and stare into the clear sky at the countless stars that twinkled and winked in response to my gaze. It was always has if the sky there had more stars than anywhere else on the planet and it felt like such a privilege to marvel at the spectacular sight.

Thankfully the relentless studying paid off for me and I passed the examination and was able to enrol at the college in Zagreb. Maybe this would never have been possible without the constant and unrestrained support that my sister gave me during those never ending two years and I will always feel that I owe her so much.

Before I left for college she took me on a short holiday to a hotel perched high in the mountains. She knew that I felt so connected to nature and that this would be the most perfect of places that her little sister would adore.

I remember the feeling of freedom and liberation from my studies that I felt there and was in total awe of the spectacular location in the mountains that felt so untamed and far away from the modern lifestyle. The air, the grass, the rivers all lifted my spirits to a new found high that was intoxicating in its natural beauty.

Zagreb is without doubt the most beautiful city of all the former Yugoslavia.

The lifestyle there was carefree and easy going, a far cry from the strict regime of the military academy that I had entered into.

The day there would start at 7am with breakfast. Beds would be examined by the mayor each morning and then we would be drafted into our various lessons which commenced at 8am. These would continue until 3pm and then it would be a forty minute train and bus journey to the hostel that I was lodging in. There we would eat and try to relax a little before the return journey for lessons that ran from 4pm till close at 7pm. I would return wearily to the hostel and continue with online studies into the night.

Because it was a military academy it was run with a strict military regime. At times it felt more like a hard core prison that a college and I would lie awake at night wandering just what I had let myself in for.

The weekends were my release from the strict and uncompromising torture that I was enduring and I would venture into the very heart of the city. Other students from Bosnia were there and we would meet, drink and party. Those weekends evened out the daily rigours of college life and made life there a little more tolerable.

Although I felt that I was being pushed to my very limits under the harsh regime the years seemed to glide passed and I soon found myself in my third year. Every Friday I would receive money from dad with the same message that he had been writing from the very first week "Be good and study. Love you, Dad".

Fridays were always the happiest day for me, those few same words meant so much to me as I loved my parents dearly and missed them so much.

When you are young and happy you never really think that anything can shatter your dreams and plunge you into despair.

Everything is so easy and natural. We had music and fun. Pink Floyd, Janis Joplin and Jimmy Hendrix were the gods that we looked to for inspiration. We would have concerts, play guitars and above all else have laughter in our lives.

It felt like I was in the very heaven that the biblical books wrote about and like most teenagers I never questioned if this would come to an end.

Pink Floyd wrote "Now there's a look in your eyes, like

black holes in the sky". My own black hole came the day that I was jolted back into reality.

I was told that granddad had died. I could not take this in and thought over and over that no, there was some mistake. He could not die, he would live for ever because that was the sort of figure that he was. It slowly sank in that, yes he was dead and I remember the utter feelings of guilt and remorse that engulfed me. I felt helpless and so selfish that I had not visited him in four years. He had died there whilst I was here, enjoying life so carefree, and lost in my own world of laughter, music and happiness.

I was told seven days after his death and after the funeral. My family thought that this was the best way has they did not want my schooling to suffer with me taking vital time out to travel to Bosnia.

At night I would lie awake and cry myself to sleep. Tears would flow in a never ending stream of sorrow. I remember thinking that I would never again be the subject of his wise and knowing advice. His addictive laughter and jokes. I was constantly drawn back to my last visit to that beautiful place. He called out as he saw me approach "Hey Petra you came, did you bring me lamb meat?" I answered that no it was not mam but me. "Oh it is you Vesna, my sun you are." Those are the last words that I remember him saying to me.

It is so ironic that within twelve months the other side of the tossed coin would feel the same sorrow and utter devastation with the loss of granddads brother. The sorrow and sheer emptiness that would begin a twenty year search that would not cease, regardless of utter frustrations until both sides were at last side by side, finally being able to face the other with a long lost knowing and understanding.

Although my own sorrow of losing granddad was intense I felt dearly for mam. She loved her father with a passion. He was the only surviving family member that had escaped the night of horror back in 1941. Although he had remarried, mm and her step mother never really came to terms with each other and probably only ever tolerated each other through the love of the same man. After his death they only met to exchange monies that mam had secured to purchase granddads property and land.

With that sealed they would not cross paths again.

Following the death of granddad I was again drawn to the lost brother and wandered of his fate. Was he still living, and if he was, did he know that his own brother had died.

My sister would recall that whenever mam ask granddad about his brother Maksim, he would struggle for breath, tears would well upon his face as he bid his excuses before he left the room. It was obvious that the passing of time was not as we are told, a healer and that he missed dearly the brother that was long since gone.

Back at the academy I was beginning to enjoy the constant regime of learning. In my final year the pieces were beginning to fall into place and I now felt that I was at last achieving something.

I remember the visits to family in Bosnia and especially to those visits to my brother. He would coax me and outline that I was the smart engineer. He would fire mathematical questions at me and I was always frightened that the answers would be incorrect as he too had spent time at mechanical school.

Finally my school days came to an end with my graduation. I will never forget seeing my sister who had come to collect, me to take me home, Acoustic guitar wrapped in a huge bow. How I cried with sheer joy at the sight and we held and cried for what seemed like an eternity.

Bratstvo – Welcome to the Machine

It was so hard for me to have to say a final farewell to the people that I those long years with at the academy but regrettably, that summer it was finally time for me to leave and return to my hometown in Bosnia.

Zagreb will stay ingrained in my memories forever. Like a beautiful companion that had helped me through the strict, and disciplined regime that I had to follow throughout my studies.

The journey through the mountains passed and I felt the realisation that I was now to face the tough transition in life. From that of a carefree student idling away the summer weekends to that of a working adult and the responsibilities that this role has to carry.

It was only when I finally arrived home did I then realise just how much I had missed my family. Evenings were spent chatting and catching up on times lost whilst I had been away. Mam I remember would sit and smile as I caught he gazing lovingly at me as if she was seeing me for the very first time and would embrace me as if never wanting her baby to leave her again.

After seven years of dedication to study I wanted to stay now embraced in the love of a family that I had missed so much. This, I feared was not to be and I was expected to report for work at the Armament factory that was situated on the near outskirts of town.

The factory was colossal and employed between seven and eight thousand workers.

The reality hit me so hard as I entered through the huge gates on my very first day there. I had expected a reward of some kind after my strenuous efforts with my education, instead I felt hugely disappointed as I was herded into the huge workshop with hundreds of others starting the days work. I felt like an ant in a driven colony as I looked into the tired faces of those already used to the daily ritual.

Most of these faces I recognised from town and I was welcomed aboard with the smiles of kindness. I would smile back as the eager newcomer but deep down I was already to have regrets that I had entered such a place. Maybe, just maybe I thought, the life of an engineer was not for me despite the tremendous efforts and time that I had given to pass my grades. After all I thought, god had brought me now so far and had placed me here for a purpose.

Despite my inner reservations I held my head with pride and worked with the feverish pace and enthusiasm of youth.

Maybe my enthusiasm was to be my downfall as I was moved to the largest of the workshops where I would carryout computerised diagnostic testing on the huge machinery there. Although proud that I had been selected so early in my career at the factory I was also having the feelings of suspicion and dread. Mira, a friend at the factory would laugh and wish me good luck, she said this with a knowing smile and that began to disturb me as she knew what was awaiting me there.

I remember feeling the desolate isolation I felt as I entered the workshop that very first day. To say it was huge would be an understatement. Thousands of faces seemed to turn at me in unison as the shouting and whistling rose to fever pitch as I wearily walked down the long aisle.

The whistling and shouting continued without relent and I felt so very alone and out of my depth. I was ushered into the foreman's office and was told to ignore the mayhem around me.

The leader then took me back onto the shop floor, the shouting grew in decibels and I turned to see the horror that one of the workers had picked up a tool and was posed as if to strike the worker next to him. In sheer panic and desperation I turned and ran towards the very same door that I had entered only moments earlier.

I realised in that instant that I could not stay at the factory, that the people there were maybe a little crazy and feared that it would be only be a matter of time before behaviour like that which had been displayed would ultimately lead into someone receiving a serious injury, or worse still be subject to murder at the hands of the mob.

I remember going home that night, so frightened and alone, heart in mouth and confused.

With heavy heart and dread I would return to the mayhem and chaos each day. Never understanding the scene that was being set before me...

Each day I entered the workshop the cackles and whistles would slowly falter, something far more important than me was about to enfold. Everyone was guessing, speculating what was going on. The stories were varied and ranged from politics to trading but nobody really knew what was actually happening.

With heavy heart and fear that I was slowly turning into one of the jostling faces at the factory I continued in my work there. Although I had studied for so long to become an engineer my heart simply was not on the shop floor and yearned for something more. T fought and fought against desire but eventually its pull was too strong and I gave in and started to think of the alternatives.

I would think of the family that may be there somewhere in England and so wished that somehow, after all these years there would be a connection.

Despite my wishes the years slowly past and I became, without realising one of the oily faces of the nightmare of that first day at the factory. Three years passed before I awoke from the slumber that I had fallen into. Oh god I awoke feeling the dread that I had become. I realised that now I had to leave this place and began to plan my future away from the grimy essence of the factory and maybe away from Bosnia too.

My parents realised just how serious I was when I told them that I was going to apply for a visa and head for Switzerland where I was to stay, initially with there friends who lived there.

Did you see the Frightened Ones?

Maybe they also knew that something stirring in Yugoslavia and that it would be a wise decision for me to leave. The economy was in downfall and people were out of work like never before.

I applied for a four month visa and busied myself packing and looking closely at my options. Despite the strenuous efforts I had made to qualify as an engineer the truth was that I was not committed to this as my life long career and, even worse I did not truly know what I wanted in life.

All too quickly my stay in Switzerland came to an end with the passing of four months flashing past in the blink of an eye.

In the final weeks of my stay I began to listen to the conversations and the stories being told in the bars at night. They centred on a widening rift between the Serbian and Croatian people that was worsening daily. That Croatia wanted to break away from Yugoslavia and that Serbia was strongly opposing any move towards independence. People were advising me that I should not return to Bosnia and that I should look at other alternatives.

Maybe my stubbornness got the better of me and I put these stories to the back of my mind and returned to my home town.

I remember walking through the town that I had been raised and knew so well. In the short space of my four month absence something there had changed. Something was unfolding that I had no understanding of. Everyone seemed to be hurrying in their daily lives as if in great haste to complete their business. The stories of mayhem were countless and I remembered feeling frightened and for the first time in my life so very alone. A small person, standing in the middle of something so huge. I would ask what was happening but people would simply look at me as if I was from another planet. Even my family were acting strangely. I would overhear them in hushed conversation in the evenings. The talk always centred on the worsening problems between the Croatian people and the Serbs. That the economy was spiralling out of control in Bosnia and that the only way forward was for the ordinary people to look towards the private marker for employment and not to rely on the state controlled industries for security as had been the case under the old socialist federation.

As the talk and speculation continued with ever growing intensity I received a telephone call from my sister Mira. She had lost her job in the never ending stream of unemployment and warned me that things were only to become worse in the weeks that were to follow. She went on to say that all businesses in the surrounding areas were turning to the private sector and we too had no alternative to follow the same route. She was adamant that for the family to survive the impending doom we too must look at investing the money we had into a private enterprise and the best option open to us, given the limited investment available was to rent a suitable building where we could operate a wholesale and retail store for cheap and affordable clothing. Something that, despite the worsening economic climate, people would always need.

The following few months saw Mira's advice turn into reality. We pulled together our resources as a family unit and secured a suitable address in which to operate. The days were excruciating long and hard but eventually we found ourselves making slow headway in the rapidly declining transition from socialism to capitalism.

Although the stories were now of open warfare on the Croatian – Serbian border we put these to the backs of our minds and focused all of our efforts in making our small family enterprise a success. After all, the border was distant and, with foolish hindsight, we wrongly thought, would not affect us in Bosnia.

Following the initial enthusiasms and progress we soon found it ever increasingly difficult to find a ready market for the clothing that we needed to turn over to provide us with income in order that we could continue trading.

In order for us to continue where others around us were failing in business we were forced to travel around to find the buyers for our wares. It became a tortuous ritual of travel and sell. The days were never ending as we covered the markets from Belgrade to Zagreb. We would simply drive through the night and promote our goods during the day. It was a never ending and exhausting cycle that we had to pursue in order to simply survive.

With the ever pushing desire to keep our heads simply above water we carried on the daily ritual of work, work, work and became oblivious to the danger that was settling all around us.

Fierce fighting was widespread on the border regions, the same borders that had been invisible since 1945.

Despite the ever increasing envelope that we had surrounded ourselves it was slowly dawning on us that just maybe we were not as immune to the rising tensions that were escalating in our country. As the days passed it was all too apparent that the civilian traffic on the roads was dwindling, to be replaced by the sheer might of military hardware.

One night in particular brought us crashing to the ground to face openly that just maybe we were not the most important thing and that our tiny enterprise was punitive with retrospect of what was really being unleashed and, worse, was about to unfold.

As was the usual for our accustomed routine we were driving through the night to our next destination that we might be able to exchange goods for currency. The road, which cut through dense woodland, was particularly dark and, rounding a sharp corner we were forced to swerve sharply to avoid a military roadblock. The car came to a shuddering halt and we were faced with the formidable sight of a huge armoured tank within inches of our own punitive, in retrospect, mode of transport. Given the David and Goliath comparison, it was in no ones doubt who would have been the overall winner had there been an outright collision between the two.

In blind panic we tried in desperation to turn the car around and were immediately halted by the sharp and final orders to stop by the military figure, pistol in hand, that was illuminated in the cars headlamps. He ordered us to get out of the car and asked where we were headed. We explained that we were driving to Belgrade in order that we could trade there. He looked at us in sheer amazement as if we were crazy. With a shrug of his broad shoulders he waved for us to return to our car and turned round with a shake of his head.

Realisation was dawning on me for the rest of our journey. The idle conversations and tales of dread had truth in them.

Evil was lurking slowly but surely across Bosnia and its spread could not be stopped. Within weeks of that sobering encounter in the woods with the tank Novi Travnik was slowly being sucked into the abyss that was approaching.

There were strangers in town with so much hate in their eyes as they glared, scanning everywhere and everyone. I would hurry through the streets in fear of these strangers and would not venture out after dark. Others felt this too and I remember listening through the apartment window and heard only the echoes of the empty streets. The same streets that only months before had been filled with footsteps and laughter.

Occasionally I would be woken with a start in the early hours to the sound of shouting and the violent banging on neighbours doors. Gunshots would be heard and the stories of robbery, violent beatings and rape were becoming more and more. The strangers with hate in their eyes were now the law. They could do as they pleased and no one could stop them. With this knowledge the horrors worsened and even daylight was no longer a welcoming sight, no longer a brief respite from the nights of dread and fear.

Soon even worse news began to filter its way through. Open warfare had started in Sarajevo to the south. This was warfare however with a difference. Civilians were being targeted and the horrific details of mass murder and mutilation were countless.

My own town was becoming a breeding ground of hatred and revenge. I have never felt fear like I felt at that moment and so desperately wanted to leave the horrors and barbarity behind.

I again thought of granddads brother in the safety and luxury of England. If only I knew that he had family still living maybe we could reach them and flee to safety. I did not know however so for the time being was forced to stay and face the daily strife regardless.

Hatred would rear its head constantly and neighbours, friends and even families would be torn apart by its vile presence. People that had loved each other only months ago would attack, maim and even kill there new found enemies. Horrors became just part of a normal day and people would simply look in the other direction when scurrying through the streets.

Refugees from Sarajevo flooded into the town and the whole place looked as if was a casting place for extras for some multi million pound war movie. The scene was unreal and I would shake my head as if to rouse myself back into reality.

The refugees would speak of their own horrors that that had witnessed first hand. They told of the city being totally cut off from the outside world. They spoke of artillery and mortar attacks that were being aimed at the thriving market places where civilians packed into to try and buy the dwindling food stocks to feed their hungry families. They had escaped in time before the final escape routes had been sealed and the people that remained were now helpless to defend themselves from the vicious onslaught.

Within days of the first arrivals a convoy of busses arrived in town. The passengers were packed tightly and they were all children. Their faces looked out with the look of despair that was unimaginable. These were the faces of emptiness and lost hope. They were the children of Sarajevo whose parents were condemned to stay in the dying city to face their own horrors.

Everyone crowded the buses to take the children to the safety of their homes.

I embraced a boy and a girl, brother and sister. We cried so much as we held each other so tight. We would give them food and shelter overnight before they continued their own sad and harrowing journey to safety. It was so dreadful to think as you looked into those helpless and innocent eyes that some, if not most were already orphans, without them actually knowing so.

The next morning was so sad to see the children being returned to the convoy of busses and to watch them wave in sadness as they were driven out of town.

I later learnt with great sadness that the convoy never reached its destination and that the vehicles were never to be seen again.

I look back now and it amazes me how the human mind can adapt itself to the situations around us. There I was struggling from day to day in my own survival whilst witnessing the horrors and brutality that was being played out every minute of every day.

Every vile and inhuman act of savagery I would fold away in the back of my mind as if it had never happened. I knew that for my own survival I had to remain strong and continue the tortures of simply living. Then it becomes a struggle to stem back the flood of what is witnessed and this adds to the weight that you have to endure. The mind is built for survival and it is this primeval instinct that would carry me through the next four years of warfare and sacrifice.

I remember one day in particular. I had ventured outdoors to visit a friend who lived nearby. As we chatted in her apartment we began to hear footsteps and raised voices coming from the town square below. Curious we stepped onto the balcony to see what was happening and were met with the spectacle of soldiers in black uniforms standing in rows. At the forefront was their commander who was bellowing out orders. Although I could not hear what was being spoken I knew by the response of the black uniformed audience that it was not a Sunday sermon. They would yell and whistle in agreement and has the crescendo reached fever pitch they began to fire their weapons into the air.

In panic and desperation we ran from the balcony into the apartment, closing and locking the door as if this simple act would keep us safe from the anarchic scene below. We stayed there huddled together in prayer and, as darkness fell the nightmare began.

Outside we could hear the heavy sounds of people running. The footsteps became louder and we knew that they were coming from in front of the apartment block. Then came the frightening booms of gunfire and the deafening explosions that rattled the very foundations of the building. I remember the feelings of utter terror when the realisation broke through that open warfare had arrived on the streets of Novi Travnik. I wanted to crawl away and hide but realised that I was trapped amongst the carnage and murder. Sounds of breaking glass resounded from below and I knew that apartments were being trashed by the unknown assailants. The scene repeated itself throughout the night, running footsteps, shattering glass, gunfire and the screams that chilled the very soul. Although I am not naturally a religious person I sat in that small room and prayed like I had never prayed before.

As daybreak slowly beckoned the noises gradually lessened and then came the eerie silence of normality.

I remember the scenes of utter destruction as I speedily ran through the empty streets to get to my families apartment. Buildings were burning and the stench clawed at my nostrils. I was fighting for breath but my legs refused to give in to exhaustion and before I knew anything else I was home and leapt into my mam's open arms struggling for breath and battling away the tears and sobs that racked my already exhausted body.

That night was just the beginning of the fresh horrors of what become a daily ritual of murder and survival. I so desperately wanted to escape the living hell but there was no way out. In stark realisation I realised that returning to my homeland had been a grave mistake and that I was now destined to face my own consequences, whatever their outcome would be.

Humanitarian organisations set up shelters all across town and offered food rations and I would watch the faceless queue with tears of sorrow and pity. Each day I would notice the absences of people that I had known and each time I would fear the worst. That they now had become merely a statistic, in the enveloping madness that had the town in its deadly grip.

Like those around me I had become merely a face in the crowd of sadness and desperation. At night I would lay awake and cry myself through the long hours. Everything that I cherished had gone, the beauty that had surrounded me as I had grown in this town had slowly sank into rot and decay as I stood helpless and alone.

Loneliness is probably one of the hardest crosses that we can ever bear. One of the deepest and strongest emotions is for the human mind to feel the need to belong and to be part of society.

One of the worst things that can happen is for us to be rejected by the same society that had nurtured you and loved you as its very own.

I remember the feelings of utter and total despair when this happened to me and my own family. It was if we simply did not belong amongst those that we knew and the surroundings that we were accustomed. We had suddenly lost all feelings of self value and were left hoping that one day we would again find our place amongst the people around us.

I was learning so fast how hatred can spread its vile web into the very core of the human body and soul. How religion and language can manifest itself into a reason to kill and torture.

I would see daily how older, respected individuals would feed this vile hatred into the minds of the younger ones who would kill and maim in the cause that they had been so misled to be right and just.

I look back and think of those people that brought so much bloodlust and carnage to the ordinary people and wander if they ever ask themselves the simple question of why? Do they have remorse for there actions and will they live there own natural lives carrying the heavy burden of what they had contributed to and had taken part.

With little hope and the chance to make life a little more bearable I decided to return to work at the armaments factory.

There was little else left now in the town and at least the sporadic wages would help ease the pain of day to day living and despair.

We assemble at the factory gates at 7am each morning and pray as we rounded the corner that the same flag as the day before would be fluttering in the breeze. Usually it was not and this meant that now one of the other warring factions was in control of the area for that day.

Each day too the workforce was rapidly diminishing in numbers. The falling numbers was not a gradual decrease but would be dwindling by the hundreds and all manner of horrific stories on the shop floors were being relayed for the countless absentees.

As well as work at the factory I would also continue to help my family at the clothing boutique. Operating and running a store that has no customers had become a daily routine for many traders in the town but the slightest hope of just one sale was enough to make it all the worth while.

I remember one day in particular when I had offered to cover for one of the assistants who wanted time away.

As usual the store was empty of customers and I was counting the hours until it was time to leave. Unexpectedly the door swung open and in stepped a black uniformed soldier, machine gun in hand. He swaggered towards me with an air of complete arrogance and I was shaken to the bones when I looked into his eyes. They were the eyes of utter and complete lack of human emotion but, not wanting to show that I was frightened by this opposing barbarian figure I stepped up politely and asked defiantly if he was looking for anything in particular. He beamed down at me, maybe a little surprised and told me that he needed jeans. As I searched the racks for his size again the door swung open and there stood another black uniformed thug, again with machine gun hanging loosely at his side. This one was laughing uncontrollably and was obviously looking for fun or trouble. Hurriedly I found the correct size and passed him the jeans. I was shaking so much but knew that to show fear then the pair had won and this could heighten their bravado and place me in more danger than I know was. Instead I asked, rather stupidly perhaps, if there was anything else that he wanted. Sneering in my direction he snarled that yes, maybe there was something else here that he would love dearly to try on. His crudeness only exasperated the others manic hysteria but I stood politely in defiance my ground without showing either fear or weakness.

They were backed into a corner now and unsure of my own nationality because the boutique was in the "right side of town". Had this not have the case then It is highly likely that I would not have been left alone, frightened by the experience, and that this story would never have been told.

In those dark times I remember also my little car. When I had finished college I had begged and begged my father to buy me a car. I was, after all an adult I would explain to him, and needed transport of my own. In the end his love for me gave way and I had the car. A little Fico. Oh how I loved that little car. It was the best present ever, forgetting of course, the little pull along dog from so long ago. My little car brought so much fun and freedom. I recall, having five people crammed into its tiny interior, all laughing with the carefree days of no tomorrows.

I awoke one morning and the car was gone. Empty was her allotted space and she was no more. How empty I felt walking the war torn streets for her comfort but there was none. My little Fico had been stolen away from me as I slept.

Days later I found my little Fico. She was parked outside one of the existing cafés that remained open. Sat drinking coffee as if everything around them was normal and that they were simply taking morning coffee were the black uniformed militia that were in control again for that day.

How I looked at my little car as I hurried past. So sad for my own loss but even sadder for the poor wretches that, now drinking coffee knowing that she was theirs. They were sad figures in their own right, they were together, rifles and grenades in hand, but, how sad, and they still felt the need for that little Fico to make them feel macho and whole.

War is a pure example that nothing materialistic in our lives is important. Like my little Fico, I no longer cared. I would pray over and over again that the fighting would stop and life would resume to normality. My prayers were on hold and the peace never came with the dawning of a new day.

Bratstvo – The End of the Dream

I will never forget that first day when I was truly exposed to the horrors of modern war.

As usual I was woken by dad's call that it was time to go to work. Oh how I grown to hate those words. What was the point I would think. Production was almost at a standstill and we were not even receiving our wages. Despite this my parents were from a generation when punctuality and reliability meant everything and, they would constantly point out that after the fighting the factory would continue to operate and that management would favour those that had remained loyal through the difficult times.

Eventually, as always I gave in to his calls and dressed. Mam had made breakfast as usual but I could not eat. I felt sick and had pains in my stomach.

As usual I kissed them both goodbye and set out on the forty five minute walk. It was a beautiful August morning and I absorbed its beauty, the sun was shining and the birds were chirping as if all was normal, that war was only a thing of memory and past.

Once at the factory the day started as usual. There was little work to do except maybe go over some old blueprints and make slight modifications.

As lunch time approached the pains in my stomach were becoming unbearable and I decided that I could stand the pain no longer and would leave for home.

My building was on the far upper part of the factory next to the second exit. As I was about to exit the building I heard a terrifying loud explosion and felt the ground shudder as if we had been hit by an earthquake. All people around me just froze on as the whole building swayed as if it would fall to the ground. We kept looking at each other in shock and somebody yelled "everyone run, we are being bombed". I could not believe what was happening and felt that I was caught up in some collective nightmare that was being shared by everyone that was around me.

Everywhere was panic and mayhem and I remember running and screaming so loud that it felt that my lungs would burst from the sheer strain of my exertions. Over the screams and crashing of people colliding with machinery I heard the terrifying sound of airplanes. Screeching so low and fast and then the deafening sound of the explosions as the bombs found their targets and unleashed the horror for which they had been designed.

In blind panic I stopped running and stood amidst the carnage and cried for my mam. Just as I was to abandon all hope of ever getting out of the factory alive I remember feeling the strong arms of another worker grab hold of me and pull me along as he ran towards the exit and then shoved me into his parked car. He told me to sit tight as he accelerated and weaved his frantic way through the rubble and debris that, only moments ago had stood as a monument to the rising glory of the new Yugoslavia, the very symbol of its hope and forecast prosperity.

To this day I do not know who my rescuing saviour was that day and I so wish that he remained safe through the following years. Maybe one day our paths will cross again and I am able, at last to tell him how very much I remain indebted to his bravery that had probably saved my life.

The same scenes of horror met us as we speedily drove into town. Four aircraft were screaming low over the buildings and discharging their deadly cargo in a hail of thunder and fire. The scene was that of a heavily financed movie and not that of real life. How could this be happening I repeatedly asked myself? How can man have so much hatred that he could do this to his fellow man?

As we rounded a sharp corner I asked if I could be let out of the car as I needed to find my family. He stopped and in panic and desperation I leapt from the vehicle and ran as fast as my aching and trembling legs could carry me.

I ran to the family boutique which thankfully had escaped intact. My friend was sheltering inside the store and told me that she had not seen any of my family and that they must be taking shelter at the apartment. In blind panic I dialled the family telephone number. Luckily it rang and mam answered. She was crying and screaming so much that I could not understand anything that she was saying. I repeatedly told her, through my own panic, to calm down and to listen to what I was saying. I told her that I was safe and so too was Mile, my brother. I lied about this as the last time I had seen Mile was as the bombs were falling on the factory, but if I had told her that I did not know his whereabouts then this would have added to her panic. I then telephoned my sister. She too was crying hysterically and told me that a bomb had exploded in front of her own apartment and that her husband was injured. With this she hung up.

The airplanes approached yet again and the noise was deafening. I knew that I needed above all else to be with my family and set out, running through the street. I was in a nightmare I realised that there would be no waking from. The streets were full of debris and shattered glass and I passed charred ruins that had taken direct hits. Sheer desperation kept me running when my body told me that it had suffered enough. The adrenalin had taken over and I knew that I had to run and that I could not stop until I had reached the family apartment.

I burst through the door into the living room and mam ran at me and held me so tight. Tears were streaming down her face and she was relieved when I lied again that Mile was safe, that he had called into the boutique and that I had spoken to him. Dad was stood on the balcony, hands outstretched and shouting to the planes overhead "How can you do this to the people? You are bombing the factory when you know that it is full of innocent people."

Mam was horrified when I said that I was leaving to check on Mira. She begged me not to go back out onto the streets but I side stepped her and left the building. Again I pushed my already exhausted body past its own limits and before I knew anything else I was inside Mira's apartment. I was horrified to see that her husband was covered in blood. He was wearing a white jump suite and this only exaggerated the crimson blood that covered him from head to foot.

He too had been stood on the balcony, staring in disbelief at the scene unfolding before him. One of the aircraft had come in low over the buildings and had shed its cargo of death, narrowly missing the apartment building. Outside there was a huge crater which was at least half the size of the whole building which contained four hundred individual apartments.

Nothing could have ever prepared me for the horrors of that first day of air strikes. Maybe my life there in the factory had been saved by the pain in my stomach that had troubled me throughout that catastrophic morning. Had I not been in so much pain and had decided that I was to leave the workshop and head for home the story just might have been very different and I could have been just one more sad statistic of Bosnia.

What had happened on that day had been an inhumane act of cowardice that only strengthened my own resolve to live through the nightmare and I was filled with the determination that regardless of what was thrown at me and the people that I loved and cared, I would continue with the pride and dignity that the attackers had so desperately wanted to strip away.

I lay awake that night reliving over and over what I had seen and experienced that day. I was in the midst of a waking nightmare that repeated itself over and over in my mind. The drone of the aircraft continued long after they had finished the job that they had set out to do and returned to their safe bases in Serbia. Years later the sound of aircraft passing innocently overhead would ignite those awful memories from the nightmare and I would be sent tumbling back in time to relive that long gone, summers day in August.

That terrible day sparked an exodus of people that were finally leaving the town. The day of my own departure finally arrived after I received an invitation from a friend in Belgrade to stay with him there for as long as I wanted. He had heard of the horrors that were spreading throughout Bosnia and said that he would welcome both me and a friend as a guest.

Within two days we were ready to leave and secured tickets for the bus that would take us to the safety of Serbia. I later learnt that the bus we had travelled was the last one allowed to leave Novi Travnik and, any person that wished to leave the town would have to obtain permission to do so from the military authorities.

It was a terrible thing for me to do, leave my family behind. Leaving loved ones is always difficult but to leave them in the middle of a war zone is probably the hardest thing I have ever had to do in my whole life. As the tears flowed with the hugs and kisses I wandered deep down if I would ever see them again.

Standing, waiting for that bus to arrive I prayed that my family would be safe and, looking up into the clouds, I also wandered now if god had any more surprises in store for me or, if I were now to be left alone, to live my life now without further suffering and distress.

With one final look back at the town that I knew I wished dearly that I would never have to return, that our paths would never cross again and that a safe new start was waiting for me in Belgrade.

As the bus moved slowly on I withdrew deeply into my own thoughts. I was living amongst the scenes of some huge blockbusting movie and searched for the answers that would create the next instalment, the final chapter.

In the modern world of DVD rental all too often we are given the choice, an active part in the movie. Do we sit and watch the true ending to the film, or the alternative. Rocky Balboa gave us the choice, we could sit and watch the age old hero finally be defeated or, with the simple flick of a switch, we could watch him, with fondness, defeat the aggressor despite the apparent, overwhelming odds.

My own life at that time was like the tragedy that I hoped the flicking of alternatives could be switched to open up another final chapter of happiness and belonging.

Regardless of my own thoughts the bus weaved its way through the once beautiful regions of Bosnia. My relief turned into dread as I saw the carnage and utter destruction all around me. Wherever I looked the horrific scene was always the same. Houses had been destroyed, whole villages that we drove through were deserted and derelict as if some mystical force had simply removed everything living and left the structures to burn and rot. Burnt out vehicles littered the road and the bus driver struggled relentlessly to keep his own living passengers moving through the hell that had descended all around.

The horrors now of the first air strikes against my own town seemed almost trivial to what was being opened up with the passing of miles. This was destruction and human madness at its very worst. If there were a living hell here amongst us in the modern world then, I thought here it was, for all to witness its testimony and vile agony.

As the pain naturally numbed my brain to the fresh horrors that each corner of the road enticed my gaze I wandered deeply how could such a thing happen. How the rest of the world could sit and watch in the comfort of easy chairs and surround sound television, whilst the people of Bosnia were succumbing to madness and slaughter.

I would think again to the lost brother of granddads in England, was it possible that he still lived to watch the carnage of his birthplace repeat itself yet again and, if not, was there still a deep connection there that was giving thought to the pain and suffering that was being felt by its own people left behind so long ago.

Slowly, ever so slowly the fires and suffering subsided and we left the glowing embers of Bosnia behind, with great relief to everyone on board.

The driver of the bus was signalled to pull over by the roadside at a military checkpoint. Formidable, expressionless border control personnel entered the bus and scrutinized closely everyone aboard and their belongings. Men were led off the bus to undergo more in depth examination and questioning until; finally the bus was waved its all clear, and was allowed to cross the invisible line that meant safety and Serbia.

Once across the border we made our way to the house that we had been invited to stay for as long as we desired. Once there the family welcomed us with open arms and made us comfortable in their home. We stayed with the family for two days before we left and travelled south to the second house that they owned and used for vacations.

Once there everything seemed just too good to be true and I remember pinching my arm to make sure that I was experiencing some idyllic dream and would not awake to the sound of planes and exploding bombs. The neighbours were an old couple and welcomed us each morning with something freshly cooked for breakfast. The dream continued and I felt the pangs of guilt that here I was, safe and in beautiful surroundings whilst those that I loved were trapped in the bloodshed that had swept across Bosnia.

On the fourth day we were startled with heavy hammering on the door. Once opened I was shocked to see three men, all with long hair and beards. They had the same look in their eyes that I had first seen in the faces of the black uniformed thugs in my home town and this sent a shiver down my spine.

One of the men put his foot in the doorway and asked coldly "Are you Serbs, Orthodox?" Quite stupidly I asked back that it did not matter what nationality we were. The men were obviously shocked at my response and the aggression in their expressions manifested itself instantly. Quickly I blurted out that yes of course we were Serbian and also that we were of the Orthodox religion.

This eased the tension immediately and an eerie smile spread across their faces in unison. The one that had spokes told us that tonight they would take us out and that we must be ready when they would return later. I realised in that instant that we had not simply been asked out on a date and that this was an order that we must obey or reap the consequences.

Nervously that afternoon we got ourselves ready for the uncertainty that was to follow in the evening. We were so frightened and froze when at 6pm the same thundering knock bellowed from the front door. The three bearded men were there and dressed this time in some kind of crude military uniform. They beckoned us in to their waiting car and drove us into the small town where we were taken to a bar that was thundering out heavy music.

As we sat at the nearest available table I noticed, with sheer horror that each one of the men were armed and had grenades hanging from their belts.

I knew that we were in the gravest of danger and that we should do nothing to upset our "dates" and that we must pretend that we were enjoying their company and make out that we were by choice rather than because we had simply been told to do so.

Fear is a difficult emotion to win over and overcome regardless of how many times that you experience its true horrors. I found on that night however, that it can be overcome and that the human mind is built for survival and when the time comes it will resort to anything in order for it to continue its existence. I agreed with anything they said in order to make them feel that I truly liked them and was honoured to be in their company.

With agonising cruelty the evening wore on until finally the leader of the three, the one who spoke at the house bellowed out that he was sick of this stupid place and ordered everyone to leave. I knew in that instant from the madness that glistened in his eyes that something terrible was going to happen. Like frightened schoolchildren waiting to be punished we followed them outside to the car. Before climbing into the car himself, the leader slowly unclipped a grenade from his waist and threw it into the entrance to the bar. Before it had found its target he leapt into the car and with wheels screeching, we careered wildly away from the thunderous explosion.

They were laughing hysterically as if fuelled by some potent drug that had induced insanity and evil. Fear was ebbing its way over me and I fought desperately to keep it at bay. These men were well capable of killing and had just proved that they held no limits as to what they could do and I knew deep down that the killing of two innocent women was well within their grasp.

For what seemed like an eternity the car was driven through the streets at speed until finally it came to a stop outside a house. We were ushered out of the car and into the houses gloomy interior.

I remember whispering to my friend to agree with anything that they wanted and that our very lives now depended on how we would react to the situation before us.

Once inside we were told to sit and accepted the drink offered with trembling hands.

With menace and scorn in his voice the leader leaned over and asked if we were from Bosnia and if we were Muslim. I again stated that we were in fact of the Orthodox faith and that the people of Bosnia are varied and follow many faiths not just the Islamic one.

The whole night was full of sickening questioning and veiled threats and I knew that I must remain sober and coherent if we were to survive the nightmare that had unfolded with that simple knock on the door of the house.

Maybe the gods were looking down at us that night and had decided that we had endured enough because our lives had been spared and with the rising sun we were allowed to leave and return to the house in which we were staying.

We walked in silence and once there tumbled into bed. I slept the whole day as if my body was repairing itself from what it had endured.

The following afternoon I telephoned mam to make sure that my people there were safe. Maybe she recognised the fear within my voice or maybe it was the close connection that unites a family but she knew that something bad had happened to me and she urged me to at least think about returning home.

Deep down and with deep sadness I knew that the safety of Serbia had been nothing more that a dream that I had held. I also knew that our ordeal that night would not be an isolated incident and the three men would return. We had escaped with our lives but I knew that maybe next time we would not be so lucky and that we were totally helpless in their hands.

With heavy hearts and a fear of the unknown in front of us we chose to return to Bosnia, to face whatever demons that were waiting us there. We headed north to Belgrade and gave the family our grateful thanks at their attempts to save us and handed back the keys to the house that they had provided.

Next day we got on the bus that would take us back over the border, back into the madness that my country had become.

The slow drive towards Bosnia was impeded every couple of miles by constant stops at military check points. The bus and its occupants would be thoroughly searched for weapons or anything else that could contribute and aid in the rising levels of violence and bloodshed that had smothered the land before us.

The road was littered with military vehicles that stretched right up to the border as if in some morbid show of sheer strength.

Once across the border things worsened. Again the bus would be constantly stopped and searched. This time however the searchers were not regular soldiers and were more like the extras from some unrealistic Rambo movie. They wore bandanas and masks and it was as if they were competing against each other to see who could instil the most fear into the buses occupants.

The bus rumbled on regardless and I remember being

startled from semi-slumber by panic stricken cries from the front of the bus. Straining to see what was happening I saw, with fear that we had again been stopped at a check point. This time however I knew however that we were in a far graver situation than we had faced at the previous checkpoints. This was manned by the infamous Bosnian elite paramilitary that wore the berets of their particular detachment. They were notorious and feared for their complete and utter disrespect for human lives and the stories of their atrocities were countless.

Deep down I knew in that instant that we would never see the other side of the checkpoint and began to ready myself for the worst. Amazingly I was startled from my thoughts with the sound of laughter. I looked forewords in disbelief and saw that some of the militia were laughing and shaking the hands of one of the other passengers. Amazingly I recognised her as the wife of a well known comedian from the town of Travnik. Her famous husband had been waiting at the checkpoint for her and in the excitement of being graced with such a high profile figure the militia men opened up the checkpoint and waved the bus through to continue its journey.

Fatigue and the minds own natural defence system must have finally put my body into automatic drive and the rest of the journey now seems a distant memory, a blur that passed in the blink of an eye.

As if by some magical force I landed at my parent's apartment and remember the tears of joy as mam held me tightly in the safety of her bosom as if she was holding the crying little girl from long ago that had bruised her knees from a fall in the streets. Finally the hugs and tears of a family once again united subsided and after a hastily cooked supper I withdrew to the comfort of the familiar bed that I had left behind in the hope of a better, more normal life across the border.

Next morning mam spoke to me of the possibility of me travelling to the safety of Croatia. She said that one of our neighbours had moved there before the hostilities had begun and had settled in the coastal town of Split. I did not want to leave my family again and told mam that I would hear not of it and my place now was here with the family that I lived, regardless of the perilous situation that we were facing.

Later that day I visited my sister. Mira explained that in order that the family to survive we needed money to buy the essential items that were now becoming so scarce and had spiralled in price. She went onto explain that the only way foreword now was for us to leave for Croatia as everyone in Bosnia was out of work and that no jobs could be found anywhere in our country.

Eventually, and with great reluctance I succumbed to the family's persistent advice that travelling to Croatia was the only way foreword for the family was for me to once again leave my home town and attempt to tap into the clothing market in Croatia, after all, why try and sell fashionable garments in a town that people could even buy the basic necessities for survival.

Within days I had arrived in Split. With great kindness our once neighbour offered for me to stay with him and his family in their apartment. Jure was a great guy and I love him dearly, but how he could talk and talk without stopping, even to breath. The constant talk would become a nightmare and day after day I would have to endure the constant retelling of stories that were repeated each and every day in the apartment and, at times I wandered how Jure's wife and children could endure such vocal torture as part of everyday life. I relayed to my sister that I could not tolerate the constant bombardment of the repetitive and never ending anecdotes. Mira recommended that maybe we should include Jure in our enterprise; at least if he was kept busy then he would have less time to constantly talk.

Unfortunately Mira was wrong. Now I was not only confined to the apartment where his never ending stories of fun, mirth and memories ruled supreme. Now I would have to face the barrage whilst I struggled with establishing a foothold in a strange place for the family business too.

I was in a strange town and did not know my way around. Jure was at last useful here with only the slightest of problem. He could not tell left from right so he would direct me around the streets using his watch, which he wore on his left wrist. One day however he forgot his watch. Pandemonium ruled on that day and we rarely found ourselves at the places that we had intended and trade was slow to say the least.

Even whilst we were conducting business with a prospective customer, Jure would speak non-stop. Often the customer would become so distracted they forgot their reason for the transaction and we would be left empty handed with nothing to show for our efforts.

One day things finally came to a head and I asked him simply not to speak at all, to let me continue, in utter peace and quiet to carry out the days transactions. I remember Jure replying in all honesty and sincerity that he could not remain silent and that he had an uncontrollable inner drive to talk and that he simply could not control this need to hear his own voice.

From that day I decided that the only way that I would be able to scratch a living was to go alone. Croatia was not the gold paved place that my family had believed and the same economic problems had found themselves here as well as in Bosnia.

Without Jure's directions I struggled to find my way through the streets of Split although I revelled in my new found silence. One day whilst hopelessly lost I was stopped by a Police car. The officer walked in never ending circles around by car and was laughing. The laughter disturbed, and frightened me so I asked why I had been stopped. The officer simply looked at me and told me that he had recognised the cars registration plate and that not only was it a Bosnian registration but also from the same area as he had once lived. I was so relieved and, after chatting for a while, agreed that maybe we would meet up and that he would take me out to one of the bars in town.

Maybe I made a mistake with agreeing to that meeting

for a drink. As the weeks wore on he became almost obsessed with me and would call to see me daily. His invitations to take me out turned into what seemed like orders that must be obeyed and I became increasingly worried for my safety if ever I refused. Eventually I relayed my fears to my sister during one of our regular telephone conversations and expressed my deep desire to return home. Mira would have none of this and agreed that she would travel and spend time with me there.

I was so relieved when Mira arrived in Split. Jure and his family had been so kind and I will always be grateful to them, but in essence I had felt so lonely.

We would spend those cold wintry days trying desperately to sell clothing from the boutique in Novi Travnik but we were fighting a losing battle. Prospective customers would pick out our Bosnian accents and simply retract from the transaction of sale. With dignity we held our heads high but our inner selves knew the hard truth. We were looked on as lepers and the healthy people around us seemed to fear the infection that we offered.

After spending six days with me in Split, Mira had to return home to her family. With deep regret she packed up her belongings whilst I sat, saddened with the prospect of again being alone, and watched television.

News bulletins interrupted which told of a spiralling conflict between the Croatians and Muslims and that aggression between the two was spreading.

Deep shock set in as we sat in silence watching the scenes unfold before our very eyes.

Television reports indicated that Bosnia was a no go area and that the majority of the roads were blockaded by military units or local militia. We sat in silence but our thoughts were the same. The family that we had left behind were now in deep peril and, whilst we sat in relative safety, there was nothing that we could do to help them. They were isolated now, gripped by the jaws of hell.

Hours turned into days with nothing in the way of contact.

I remember Jure's neighbour coming to the apartment to tell me that my brother was on the telephone and wanted to speak with us urgently. Fearing that something was so terribly wrong I ran up the stairs to his telephone. My brother Mile was on the line and I knew instantly that this was a social call. I remember feeling that the whole world was stood still as he gave me the news, father had died. It was not the war that had killed him; he had suffered a heart attack.

I remember the numbness that crept over my entire body as I just there, so alone and frightened. By the time that I walked down the stairs and into Jure's apartment I was shaking and crying so much it was difficult to see. Mira instantly knew that something terrible had happened and rushed to me, embracing me like she always did when I was upset. She held me so tight when I finally had the strength to blurt out the news. We stood there for what seemed like an eternity, holding each other in the warm embrace of two sisters united in grief.

We knew that we had to return home straight away regardless of the rapidly growing conflict that had swept over the country. All morning we spent at the bus depot asking every driver we came across if they were heading into Bosnia. The answer was the same, Bosnia was a no go area and that only the insane would travel in that direction.

Just as we were losing all hope of ever seeing father again a man in uniform came to us and asked us if we needed transport into central Bosnia. We explained that yes we had to get there as soon as possible. He pointed to a nearby bus and explained that we were free to travel with him and invited us on board.

As we boarded I noticed that all the other passengers were soldiers and that we were the only civilians on board. This added to my already rising fear of what we might find as we entered Bosnia. Given my previous experiences my mind ran amok with all kinds of horrors that could be lurking across the border.

I was invited to sit next one of the soldiers at the rear of the bus. Once the bus started its journey the soldier broke his silence and began asking me questions. The innocent conversation soon turned into what seemed to me more like an interrogation. I felt that history was being repeated and felt the same fear that I had whilst in Serbia in the company of the three local militia men. I knew that if the truth came out that we were in fact orthodox then we would be in grave danger. Instead of telling him the truth that would fuel his rising suspicions I gave him the details of a friend who was Croatian using Carlo's family name instead of my own. He would constantly interrupt my answers to the never ending questions and his cynical laugh made me feel nauseous with fear and dread.

Once across the border the bus soon stopped at the roadside. Suspecting that something was wrong I asked my interrogator what was happening. He replied that the bus would now have to stop every few miles in order that the road ahead could be screened for possible ambush or targeted by waiting snipers. He explained that what should take five hours to complete the journey could now take two days, depending on what lay ahead and how fierce the fighting was.

The scene was repeated throughout the day. The constant questioning wore on and the bus would drive on and stop whilst the area in front of us was checked for danger. I eventually drifted into an uneasy sleep and woke feeling the warming rays of sunshine on my face. No sooner had I opened my eyes the questions resumed.

Although we had been travelling for most of the day and through the night we were still a long way from Novi Travnik and the realisation sank in that despite having to endure the journey we would not make it in time for father's burial.

My body and mind had by now reached breaking point and I only vaguely remember the rest of the two day journey through hell itself. Maybe the mind switches itself away from the reality in order for it to survive. Whatever the reason the following day is lost somewhere in my subconscious and I only remember arriving in my home town. We had missed the funeral of our own father and this weighed heavily on my conscience. The father that had raised and cared for us so very much and I had not been there to say a final farewell.

I remember stepping of the bus and then being enveloped into a darkness that smothered me. I was drawn back into reality with the ice cold shock of people packing snow around my neck to revive me from unconsciousness.

We learned from people that we met whilst walking away from the bus that things were very different now in Nov Travnik. Fierce fighting was widespread and the town was divided into two. My parents had been forced to move as their apartment had simply been on the wrong side of town and, where they now lived was virtually impossible to either get into or get out.

In desperation we headed for the family boutique in the hope that someone would be there. Luckily one of the assistants was there and gave us directions to the apartment that mam now lived.

We had to be careful that we were not seen as we made our way through the streets. Even from outside of the building I could hear the cries of grief from inside and instantly recognised these as coming from mam.

Once inside the apartment we held her as tight in our embrace as we were united in deep grief. I felt pangs of guilt rise over me as I had not been there when mam had needed me the most and this added to the deep misery that I felt deep inside of my inner self.

As the initial grieving gradually subsided we learnt that fighting had erupted during the night and that my parents were forced to flee from their apartment under heavy gunfire and grenade attacks. The fighting intensified and father began to suffer under the stress and strain that the conflict was fuelling. One morning he had called at the boutique and had complained of a pain in his chest. On arriving back at the apartment, the pain had intensified and he had rang the doorbell in the hope that someone inside would be alerted and come to his aid. Sadly, before anyone reached the door father had succumbed to a massive heart attack and could not be revived.

The days and then weeks that followed saw me slide into the very depths of despair. My resilience and spirit were all but broken and I had become a mere shadow of the happy, hippy living girl from her academy days in Zagreb. I refused to venture outside despite the constant encouragement from Mira and confined myself indoors, inside the safety and comfort of mam's company.

Eventually the blackness that had manifested itself deep inside of me subsided and I realised that in order to survive I would have to rise above the situation that I was in and live as normal as what was possible in the middle of the carnage and death that had consumed everything around me.

With apprehension I slowly opened the door of the apartment. I remember the colours and the light of a world that I had withdrawn myself from for so long. Spring was in full swing and, despite that I was in the middle of a bloody and desperate war zone I was taken a back by just how beautiful the very basics of human existence were. I marvelled at the dappled sunshine and the sheer beauty of nature and could feel the healing process racing through my mind and body.

With my new found inner strength and determination I decided to walk into town and visit the family boutique. As I walked I was horrified at the scene that unfolded before me. Buildings that I had known had simply disappeared, to be replaced by piles of debris and destruction. Almost every place that remained standing was deeply scarred from the hatred of war, windows were shattered and the sickening holes from explosions adorned the walls. I remember thinking that god had offered us paradise but, here in Novi Travnik we had chosen hell.

Once at the boutique I was told that Mira had left to get coffee at one of the few bars that had managed to continue its business. I hurried through the debris of the streets and was surprised at how quiet the coffee shop was. I had remembered this as being a busy, bustling centre for the local gossips to take stage to a never ending audience. Now it was almost deserted with maybe ten people sitting in relative silence, lost in their own thoughts of dismay and loss.

Both Mila and Mira were taking coffee and were surprised, and relieved that I had finally broke my self imposed incarceration within the walls of the apartment.

Foolishly I asked Mile where were all the people that would normally be exchanging the idle chat of town life and simply catching up on the news of the day. As usual he was quick in his response and asked me if I thought that I was still miles away in the comfort and safety of Split. He went on to say that those who remained now amongst the rubble and despair of Novi Travnik were those that were trapped there and had nowhere else to go. That the war had escalated into a full blown conflict during the time that I had locked myself away within the four walls of my safety zone and that we must hope and pray that peace came quickly before it was finally too late for those that remained.

Over the next few days I became a regular customer to the isolated coffee bar. Here I listened to the fresh horrors that had erupted in reality since my last visit and the sharing of the horrors all around with others became a comfort to me as we suffered there collectively.

It was during one of my visits to the bar affectionately and simply known as Tomato that I saw and spoke with my future husband, Tonci. He was so different from the others around. He seemed so calm and gentle, not idling away the moments relaying the horrors of war and would speak as if we were simply taking coffee and enjoying the company away from the rigours of work during his lunch break. He was the breath of fresh air that I became instantly attracted to and I would find myself seeking out his company whenever I was away from the confines of the apartment.

Mira, as sisters do, recognised my new found vigour; the spring in my step that had been lost for so long and asked me who it was that had lifted my spirits so high that the very clouds had lost the boundaries of my touch.

Failing to her persuasion to seek out the cause of my new found happiness I confided that I had began to fall for Tonci's charm and had found myself drawn to seek out his company whenever I had the opportunity.

Later that afternoon we were walking and I noticed that Tonci was ahead of us with a group of his friends. Shyly I asked Mira if we could rest a while on the bench a little further down the street from where Tonci had settled and that I did not want to appear that I was pushing my presence upon him when he was enjoying time with the people that he knew.

Like the little girl, lost in the fairytale world of love I gazed down at the ground whilst Mira and I spoke.

Finally daring myself to look upwards I noticed that his gaze was fixed firmly on that of my own. For what seemed like an age we remained locked together in the warmth embrace of mutual attraction and curiosity.

My heart thundered like a run away steam train as Tonci rose from his resting place and walked slowly towards our bench. Without taking his eyes from mine, he walked purposefully across the pavement and asked politely if he could join us. Mira gestured a welcome whilst I simply sat there, like a wild animal frozen and caught, paralysed in the oncoming beams of a car.

Whilst he spoke I realised that I was falling in love and knew that I was helpless to stop, or even slow, the emotions that were washing over me.

The next days and weeks were spent with my thought filled only with the man that I would spend every spare moment in his company. Like most men he had been drafted into one of the military units that had formed to defend the town from the encircled attackers and every moment that it was his turn to stand on the front line I would become restless in fear that the moments we had spent together may have been the last, that my moment of happiness amongst the fear and torture would be cruelly snatched away from me in a final gesture of suffering and loneliness.

When deep love flows through the soul of someone those close can feel its presence and it was not long before mam asked me who it was that was stealing her baby's heart.

I simply could not contain the words that freely flowed from me and told her about Tonci. The words came thick and fast and I remember mam telling me to calm down, take a breath and to tell her what I had on my mind. I told her that I had a boyfriend that I cared for so much and that we had been spending as much time together as was possible in these troubled times. Surprisingly mam let down the defence that she had always put around me and seemed to warm to the man that I described as if drawing a picture of him in her minds eye from what I was describing.

Mam had always held my previous boyfriends with suspicion and mistrust; they had been the easy going, carefree guys of the hippy period from the long ago happy days of the academy in Zagreb and it was a huge surprise that she told me to invite him to the apartment to meet her. After all she said if she makes my baby happy then she too is happy.

That afternoon was like the dream reverse from the nightmare that had become Novi Travnik. Tonci came to the apartment and was welcomed with open arms by mam who connected with, like I had done, instantly. The afternoon flowed in a haze of company that I loved and cherished, refreshing conversation and deep happiness. Mam, like me had taken to Tonci in an instant and had welcomed him into the family with open arms. I look back now and see that she had never shown so much happiness since before that fatal day when dad had died, the glint in her eye and the smile, had finally returned once more.

Mam's blessing was crucial to me and that night I remember crying myself to sleep as her words reverberated over and over that, yes he was such a nice man, worthy of her precious daughter.

As the love blossomed between the two of us the violence and bloodshed escalated all around.

The enemy's stranglehold on Novi Travnik tightened and the town became embroiled in a bitter struggle for survival. During the daylight hours sirens would sound relentlessly to warn of incoming mortar fire. It seemed that nothing was spared from the incoming destruction and the projectiles would be fired indiscriminately whether military or civilian. In the darkness of nightfall it would be the snipers that readied themselves to pick out anything that moved through the deserted streets. And then came the music. The enemy had installed loud speakers on the mountains that surrounded the town and would play their music throughout the night to torture us further with the depravation of sleep.

Only the rare welcome of a moonless sky would entice the condemned out of their homes to forage for food and water. We were now entombed in the living hell of what Bosnia had become.

Each day the men of the town would be summoned to where the weapons were stored and ordered to take their allotted rifle. Ammunition was becoming scarce and uniforms were almost non existent.

Once armed the men would be ordered to their positions on the front line. The bedraggled procession was the same each and every day. Months of fierce unrelenting fighting had taken an heavy toll and it was common place for some of the men to break under the strain of what they faced. They would attempt to find solace from the horror by taking refuge, hiding in basements of derelict buildings, on the roofs of the apartments where, in their desperation to escape the days fighting they would be exposed to the sharp eyes of the waiting snipers, they would even risk death by hiding in their own chest freezers that were now empty of food.

Military units were formed to find the absent men that had not collected their weapons and, once found they would be sent to the zones that would encounter the heaviest fighting. In most cases this was almost akin to passing on them a death sentence as the chance for survival would be slim.

I remember the feeling of utter abandonment that could be seen in the faces of everyone. It felt like the world had simply turned its back on Bosnia and her people, left the survivors to suffer in silence the fate that awaited us.

No longer did we see the welcoming respite that the convoys of United Nations personnel offered. No longer were we offered the much needed supplies of food and water from the world's aid agencies. We were now so very alone; we had no food or water. Electricity had become a distant memory of luxury and the very human desire to move had become restricted to the nights that even the moon had turned its back on the people below.

At times it felt we were living out a grotesque circus performance only in our circus the reward of performance was not the applause from the eagerly watching audience but the reward of finally being freed from centre stage by the death that stalked us.

Each morning the topic of conversation would be the same, who had not lasted the night and had succumbed to the barbarity of our attackers. It would not be the deaths that would arouse our intrigue, but how death had taken away the essence of human life. Had it been mortar fire, the work of the sniper or had the victims been caught trying to escape hell, executed and sent back into town for all to see.

Whatever the reasons for their sad demise the dead would be stored in the basements of the broken apartments and garages until it was safe for those who continued to survive to bury them under the relative safety of a moonless sky.

I recall in particular the desperate plight of seeing the grief of a mother that had learnt of the death of a third son. To lose one son to the horrors would be so hard to absorb by any woman that had bore and raised a child. To lose three is unimaginable and would drive anyone into the perilous depths of despair.

Despite the horror and destruction Tonci and I decided to get married. We had initially planned that we would wait until the fighting had stopped and hoped that the ceremony could take place outside. However we had heard that once last convoy was to be allowed through the siege and that young, married couples were to be given priority.

Hastily over the coming weeks we arranged our special day with the meagre scraps that could be foraged. We managed to obtain one litre of Slivovitz, $100, one pack of cigarettes and two pounds of horsemeat, which had been given to us as a wedding present.

On November 5th the simple service took place in mam's apartment. Mam and Mira were the witnesses and my brother, Mile and his wife and a friend who brought a guitar were the only people that could be packed into the tiny room. As we said our vows in the darkness the serenade was not that of bells and organ music, but that of the hidden snipers cruelly picking out their unknown, faceless targets in the blackness.

After a little singing to the chords of my friend's guitar it was time to say our farewells and leave for Tonci's apartment as was the custom following marriage, a custom that Tonci's mother insisted that we keep.

We ran in silence through the deserted streets in fear that we would be picked out by the waiting snipers who would see us as new trophies to add to their tally.

Once inside the apartment I was horrified at the sight that met me. The walls inside were riddled with bullet holes. The building stood on the very front line and was being constantly targeted. Next morning Tonci explained that at times the enemy militia would be as close as fifty metres from the apartment and would fire blindly into the windows in the hope that someone would be in the room and be dispatched.

Both Tonci and my brother Mile would be drafted daily to man the front line of the towns defence. Mile however refused to carry a weapon as he said that he did not, and would not kill another human being. Instead he went to war armed with an umbrella. Each day he would wake, get dressed and leave the apartment carrying the umbrella as if it were a rifle. Maybe it would have been a benefit to him in the rain but served no purpose in the theatre of open warfare.

Tonci was drafted into the part of town where the fighting was at its fiercest. He told us on his return that in that part of town people had been trapped in their apartments for six months. The only water that they had was from whatever seeped through the walls in the basement and they had become so hungry that they had been forced to eat the plants that they had kept as decoration inside.

As the siege continued the inhabitable places to live were becoming scarce, most buildings now had been reduced to rubble. Mile and his wife and two young sons moved into the apartment with Mam, Tonci and I. For safety against the constant shrapnel that whistled through the air we placed two freezers, covered in cloth against the window. Even during the daylight hours we were now starved of sunlight and we were hemmed in the apartment's dank interior, bumping into each other as we moved about for exercise.

Mam would busy herself making meals out of practically nothing. She always amazed me with what she produced to keep us nourished and fed.

One day in particular she was preparing the days dish when a grenade landed in front of our building. Pieces of shrapnel escaped the shield of the freezers and screeched through the room, narrowly missing her head. She was so angry, not that we had been targeted but that the attack had come at an inconvenient time and that the attackers had ruined the food that she was preparing.

Throughout those months of deep despair and anguish mam was a pillar of strength to us all. She would fill the dark, long nights were her never endless stories from world war two and what she had learnt as a child in order to survive.

Mam showed us how we could improvise candles using a

glass of water with a little oil poured onto the waters surface and then a cotton thread could be lit as the wick.

Forages for water would take place only at night under a moonless sky. It is impossible to realise just how much water you need in order to survive unless there comes a time when you have none. We would wash the laundry in plastic containers so that the dirty water could be reused for the toilets which had to be emptied by hand due to the sewers being blocked. Hygiene was at a low level and we could only afford to wash ourselves once each weekend the smell from smell from seven unwashed bodies inside the apartment with limited ventilation would permeate the air and clog our nostrils.

Every drop of water that we used would have to be found, searching blindly in the darkness and then carried hurriedly through the streets before the snipers realised that there was movement and targeted their victims. Occasionally the waiting snipers would fire blindly into the darkness in the merest hope of finding out an unseen target. They knew that we would be outside gathering water and the lightening streaks of tracer fire would whistle overhead.

As if foraging for water was not bad enough we would also have to gather wood for fuel during the freezing cold winter months. Novi Travnik is surrounded by mountains that, before the civil war had been a haven for skiing. Winters there could be extreme and bitterly cold so, in order to survive the winter we had to heat the apartment constantly. Wood was also needed to cook as electricity supplies had been cut months previously.

Collecting wood was far more dangerous than foraging for water as this had to be done during the daylight. As the supplies of wood dwindled from the ruined bombed out buildings we were forced further from the cover of town and had to venture onto the hills that the enemy occupied.

As we hurriedly chopped down the trees before the patrols could reach where we were they would fire at us from their positions and we would run, zig zag fashion, weaving a path through their line of fire.

Once cut we would load the timber onto the large robust wooden wheelbarrow that dad had made and run as fast as we could back to the apartment with our prize.

I remember one day in particular when we had risked our lives chopping and collecting firewood. We were hurrying back down the hillside towards town with our wheelbarrow laden with chopped timber when we were startled by the loud blare of a car horn behind us. I was so startled I lost control of the wheelbarrow and the precious cargo cascaded to the ground.

The car skidded to a stop by our side and the occupants got out, laughing and pointing at our desperate plight. They mocked us in our fear and told us that they were glad and happy that we had turned into animals, forced to forage in the woods for scraps of food and water. I struggled to keep my anger at bay and realised that any retaliation could result in death. They ordered us to leave the wood where it had fallen and run down the hill from the hell hole from which we had come.

Maybe there was a god after all I thought as I hurried away. Maybe he had looked down at our plight and had decided that we should be spared that day to continue with the horrors that lay before us.

Echoes – We call to you across the sky......

As the siege continued it was not only the bullet and grenade that took its heavy toll on the people of Novi Travnik. The desperate living conditions took their own toll on the condemned people of the town.

I recall with horror the day that I was combing my hair and I heard something fall out onto the chair. I was mortified to see a tiny crawling louse. My screams brought Tonci and Mile rushing into the room. How they laughed and joked at my sad plight. The more that they laughed, the more I cried. How can this be I thought. I had been dragged down so low that now my body was infested with dirty lice.

Luckily, and probably due to the fact that it was not edible, anti-louse lotion was widely available and I quickly rid my head of the scurrying invaders.

Head lice were a common feature of the siege and it had become a perfectly normal sight to see children with their heads shaved to ward off the unwelcome visitors.

Typhoid too now became a common threat amongst the living and everyone awaited its inevitable arrival as the winter gave way to the warmer climate of spring and summer. Non existent sanitation spread the deadly germs that lurked in the rotting faeces and most would succumb to stomach upsets and pain. Winter had brought upon its own horrors of suffering and now the warmer air too brought its own legacy of misery and death.

One morning I was asked by Mira to meet her at the improvised coffee bar that head been erected. There was obvious panic in her voice and I feared the worst. On the way I called at the makeshift market that struggled even to provide the bare necessities of living and bought two cigarettes at a cost of ten deutch marks. Eggs here were on offer at a price of seven deutch marks each and for the flamboyant, a jar of home made jam could be purchased for thirty deutch marks.

On reaching the coffee bar I found Mira, huddled at one of the tables in desperate tears. She explained that during the previous night military police, wearing masks to conceal their identity had knocked on the door to her apartment. Fearing that she was to be robbed Mira had firstly ran to where the money from the boutique had been stored and hid this in her underwear.

Once inside the apartment the masked visitors demanded to know the whereabouts of Darko, Mira's husband. She explained that he was away, working for the United Nations as an interpreter. They demanded that they needed to know his exact whereabouts as he had failed to turn up for military service. Again Mira explained that he had been asked to act as interpreter to the peace keeping forces of the United Nations.

The masked intruders finally accepted what Mira had told them and turned their attention to that of theft. They demanded that she handed over any money that she had in the apartment. To exaggerate their menace over Mira one of them pulled Mira towards him and brutally placed the barrel of his weapon under her chin. She had suspected when she allowed them access into the apartment that the visit would turn into a robbery so had left a small amount of cash unhidden. Mira handed over the money, and disgruntled that they had neither found her husband to punish him nor had they come across a substantial amount of money into the bargain.

I will never forget the day that I sat waiting for Tonci to return from the daily fighting on the front line of that dirty war. He had an unusual spring in his step as he approached and I asked him what was wrong. Without saying anything in reply he produced chocolate from his pockets and the beam of happiness and joy swept across his face. The war is over he repeated over and over again as if these were the only words that he knew.

How we cried as we sat there and ate the sweet chocolate, not being able to take in what was not happening, nor could we believe after so much suffering that it could ever be true.

For the first time in Novi Travnik for over twelve months I heard the beautiful song of birds and felt the cool breeze, the very essence of living that had fled the town in terror so long ago. Everyone was stunned that, what had become the daily drudge of a living hell had finally ceased and realised that now it would be a slow, painful road to normality.

Although a ceasefire had been installed it was to be a long time before the people had free passage out of the town. Aid convoys would be allowed in and out to bring in the much needed basics for living including the much needed water that we had so frequently risked our lives to collect.

Novi Travniks infrastructure and its people had been systematically and cruelly dragged into the ground and it was obvious to all that had survived the horror that it would take generations put back the fabric and trust that had not only been sustained there but had flourished once under the hopes and dreams of a new beginning.

As the book draws to a close so do my own recollections and memories of happiness, sadness and regret. Regret is a strong human emotion that is difficult to evade and my own personal regret in life is that mom stayed behind in Bosnia when I left for America. This regret will remain with me for the rest of my being, despite the knowledge that she was happy that I was leaving behind the horrors to which I had been exposed to in my own country, as I headed for a new life and, what was hoped, better times.

Thankfully, before her death she was able to meet my two young sons, Tony and Nino whilst she was physically able to enjoy their childish play and merriment.

My final words are that of a deep and heartfelt thank you to you mom for being there for me and giving me so much love in our lives together.

The memory of that will never fade into obscurity with the passing of time and it pleases me now knowing that connections have been made now, both in life, as in death.......
Your Nena.

Chapter Seven – A Time for Final Healing

MAYBE IT DOES NOT ALWAYS rain on a Sunday in Featherstone. Just maybe it is our minds and memories that select the finest or darkest moments of our existence. Our minds are so selective at times and we pick out what we really want and need to preserve and to reminisce in our later years. Maybe then we only save what we want to save for prosperity and move the discarded fragments to one side, never to be remembered, then the truth is lost forever.

In my own case it is the happy times, "Our finest hour" that are preserved to tell the story. In Vesna's case it is the happy times, tinged with the horrors of what she was exposed that tell her own story.

My own story is that of a happiness that can never be found again. It is of idyllic days spent in the summers sun, playing as children do, in the newly cut hay, natures very own playground.

Both stories however are connected through the love of two brothers that at last are reunited in their passing. Maybe now that the connection as been made then the healing process can begin.

It is often said that time heals the grieving process. In my experience this as not been completely true, time merely gives us the scope for recollection and regret. My own regrets are many, and, as the years pass, grow and continue to do so.

Probably the biggest regret that I carry with me is that I did not take grandfather up on the offer that he wished to write a book and that I should put onto paper what he was to record. The book was to be titled simply "Displaced People" and he went onto say that it would be widely read across the world. I remember that he purchased recording equipment in readiness. Unfortunately at the time I was heavily caught up in the midst of the year long miner's strike that had gripped the country and my mind was focused on my own struggle that had been forced upon me.

I suspect that grandfather had in fact carried on regardless with his project as I would see the recorder around the house from time to time. Following his death a removal workman had informed me that a piece of furniture that he was about to remove from the house had the drawer secured closed with screws. In grief I dismissed this and simply asked him to take the furniture regardless. It was only weeks later when the recording equipment could not be accounted for did the realisation sink in. Maybe he had recorded what we had desperately asked him all our lives that we had spent in his presence.

Maybe, I feel with sadness, had I not been as reckless to pass on the long awaited invitation to enter his memories then I could have reunited the two brothers to share one last, final moment together. To relive their childish antics of smoking the corn husks and secretly drinking the plum brandy in the woods around the house. Maybe, just maybe I could have put a long lost happiness back from where it came and douse down the fires of my own never knowing.

There continues to remain many questions that have not been answered and I fear now that these have been irretrievably lost to the grave. The passing of time covers, without trace its own history and only when this history is recorded can it then be passed down to the younger generations. In the case of the two brothers, sadly this has not been the case and they both took to their graves, their own separations and losses, more importantly, the very pieces that continue to make the puzzle incomplete.

The book began in innocence and unknowing. A child that held the love of an elder, and looked upon him as an invincible. As the child grew so did the invincibility of the man until finally the reality of death took its hold and sent the child on an impossible quest of hope, despair and finally triumph.

The search as been a race, a race that could only have been won by running slowly. Each fragment of information had to be stripped to its rough bareness, scrutinised and then more often than not, discarded.

Painstakingly slowly the pieces of the puzzle were collected and put together to form what we now have as a crude and fragmented picture. A picture, however that shows the lost world of a man that he would never again see, feel or experience again after the final turning of his head so long ago.

The pages have been written by two people that were magically and spiritually brought together to bring the memories of the lost brothers. Two connections that have never met from the books start to its finish. Memories have been pulled together as one to reunite the connection that had been lost long ago.

At times it has been a painful process for both to complete and record. For one the pain and grief continues for the man that he loved, the other the open horrors that Bosnia and her people suffered in those cruel years of the 1990's.

Regardless the writing continued until the storey was as complete as it ever could be. Some of what had been lost is at least preserved here in the pages for the next generations to sustain in their memory and understanding in order that the story may continue.

For me the mystery of Bosnia unfolded itself as I had always expected it to be so when I would spend the idle days of summer in the man's presence. Granddad had retained this magical land' essence within his soul and it was this that would draw me, years after his death to continue in the desperate and never ending search to uncover what may simply have not been there to see.

Like Maksim I too am now beginning to feel the peace knowing that what I so desperately searched as finally been found. The quest for what I strived is now complete as with the book that was always to be written, regardless of whom was to pen the words. I have seen, within my own vision what he would have seen throughout his life there, the rolling hills, the scattered woodland and the love of his people.

With Vesna it is from the love of her mom, Petra that has compelled her to put pen to paper. The woman who had survived the carnage of 1941, and had strived then, to protect and cherish her own loved ones until her sad and untimely death in 2007. The woman, who had not only been exposed and lived through the horrors of war, not once, but twice in her lifetime.

Petra had been the rock that that kept the family functioning in those harsh and bitter years of the civil war and it is through her own existence and memory, equally of that of Maksim's, that made this book possible to record.

Maybe now the two brothers are finally together to catch up on what they had lost and what had been taken so cruelly away from them and the people that were to remain there. Perhaps Petra, the mother who had raised the two boys single handed after Jovo, the father who had been killed in the Balkan Wars immediately prior to World War One, continues to evade the never ending need for suckling of breast milk from her boys in harsh times.

Maybe now their smiles return as they sit once again together, on the grassy slopes of Brđani, sipping plum brandy and smoking crudely made cigarettes from corn husks has they talk now of the final coming together that the book as produced.

Whatever has been written on the pages as come from the very inner self of both that have painstakingly written their words.

The book is simply an account of family lost through the problems that mankind and the world produce. History will undoubtedly repeat itself somewhere in the far reaches of the globe and another story will unfold and, maybe, just maybe, put into print similar to what is here.

Whatever the reason here is our story, our recollections, our memories that will now remain embedded for all to see and hopefully enjoy.

www.ingramcontent.com/pod-product-compliance
Lightning Source LLC
Chambersburg PA
CBHW061257280526
45784CB00002B/798